Project Management in Marketing

CIM Coursebook: Project Management in Marketing

Frank McKee
Elwyn Cox
Matthew Housden
Lynn Parkinson

ELSEVIER

AMSTERDAM • BOSTON • HEIDELBERG • LONDON • NEW YORK • OXFORD
PARIS • SAN DIEGO • SAN FRANCISCO • SINGAPORE • SYDNEY • TOKYO
Butterworth-Heinemann is an imprint of Elsevier

Butterworth-Heinemann is an imprint of Elsevier
Linacre House, Jordan Hill, Oxford, OX2 8DP, UK
30 Corporate Drive, Suite 400, Burlington, MA 01803, USA

First published 2009

British Library Cataloging in Publication Data
A catalogue record for this book is available from the British Library

Library of Congress Cataloging-in-Publication Data
A catalog record for this book is available from the Library of Congress

ISBN: 978-1-85617-715-3

For information on all Butterworth-Heinemann publications
visit our website at www.elsevierdirect.com

Typeset by Macmillan Publishing Solutions
www.macmillansolutions.com

Printed and bound in Italy

09 10 11 12 13 14   10 9 8 7 6 5 4 3 2 1

Contents

Don't forget to look at the extra online support at www.marketingonline.co.uk which includes more free mini case studies.

Foreword

THE MARKETING FRAMEWORK

Project Management in Marketing has been incorporated into the new syllabus as an acknowledgement of what happens in much of our everyday lives. It combines a series of skills, tools and disciplines that help guide us to effective outcomes. Many of the ideas and techniques will be familiar as they involve information gathering, analysis, decision making, implementation and control.

This is still very much a marketing module, with a focus on the practical application of learned skills – the project techniques are to support the marketing effort.

Let us look at a typical marketing planning cycle illustrated below (Figure 1).

When planning marketing strategy, most models will suggest that the first step is to conduct a marketing audit of where we are, what we are capable of, what our comparative position is against our competitors and what

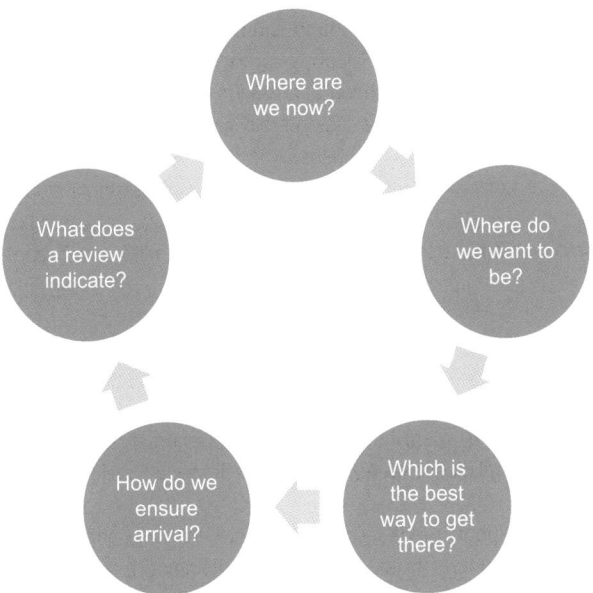

FIGURE 1

The marketing planning cycle

do our customers want from us. Any strategy must be compatible with the overall mission statement and corporate strategies that emerge from it.

To consider where we want to be is centred on segmentation, targeting and positioning (both ourselves and our offerings), in the most appropriate way to satisfy our defined target sectors.

Using a variety of tools to help choose the strategic path forward brings us to the point where we must commit resources to progress along that path. Resources are finite and valuable and whatever they are allocated to means that there is an opportunity cost – those resources are now lost to other opportunities that we may have had.

The marketing mix comprises the traditional set of marketing elements that we use, but there are further decisions to be made to achieve the best return on investment for the resources we have committed. Should we develop an online presence? Does our brand need refreshing? Has our corporate image been harmed so that public relation takes on a higher priority? These are the types of questions that may need to be answered before the best mix is agreed.

From this, our most detailed level of plan or campaign is chosen and implemented, but only the most optimistic (or foolish) organisation would imagine that everything will go to plan and at all stages. The situation is monitored and progress charted against predefined targets of success.

This monitoring and evaluation feedback cycle is a basic ingredient of most planning methods as it allows you to take corrective action to compensate for flaws in the original plan or unexpected changes in the marketing environment.

When the objectives have been achieved, for example, when market research shows that awareness of your brand has increased to the target level, then that plan is completed. This does not mean that it is completely forgotten about, but it may move to a different phase where less intensive, periodic reviews are carried out.

THE PROJECT MANAGEMENT LIFE CYCLE

If that is marketing planning in a nutshell, what is project management? A project is defined by Wysocki et al. as follows:

> *A project is a sequence of unique, complex and connected activities having one goal or a purpose and that must be completed by a specific time, within budget, and according to specification.*
>
> (Wysocki et al., 2000, p. 65)

Do the elements of that definition seem familiar? When the same authors look at the stages in a project management life cycle, they determine the stages to be as shown in Figure 2 (Wysocki et al., 2000, p. 86).

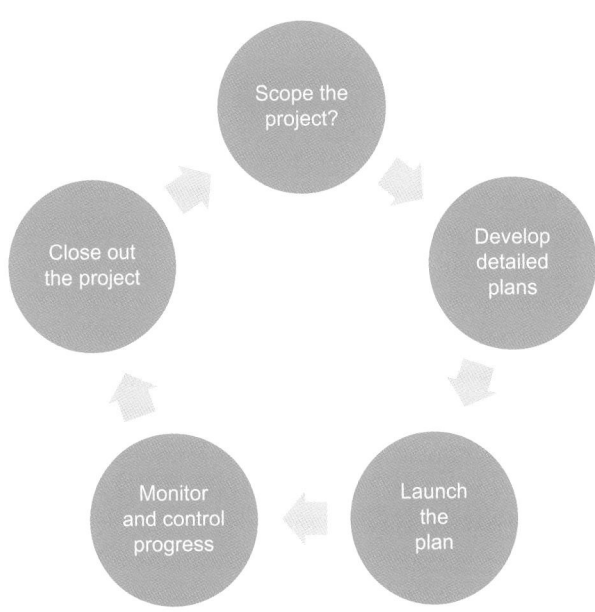

FIGURE 2

The project management life cycle
Source: Adapted from Wysocki et al., 2000, p. 86

Harvey Maylor abbreviated the stages into 4 Ds:

1. Define the project
2. Design the project
3. Do It! or Deliver the project and
4. Develop the project process

(Maylor, H. 2003, p. 28)

He illustrated these four phases with a series of key issues and fundamental questions. For the project definition stage, they included organisational strategy and goal definition – what is to be done and why is it to be done?

The design stage included planning, resource analysis and justification – how will it be done, who will do it and when can it be done?

The delivery stage includes control, organisation, decision making and leadership – how is the project managed on a day-to-day basis?

Finally, the post-delivery phase looks at developing the processes and procedures used to gain experience – what can be improved for the future?

(based on Maylor, H. 2003, p. 28)

Although many definitions of what comprises a project point out that a project is unique in nature, it does not mean that nothing *similar* has been done before. The definition is to distinguish it from routine administrative functions or closed-loop processes where identical output is the desired outcome.

A business may evaluate the level of sales on a particular product or service and choose to run a promotional campaign based on vouchers or coupons that give a financial incentive or discount. This is not the first time that they have done this for that product or service. What makes it unique is that the marketing environment and the organisation itself will have changed in many ways since the previous campaign. For example, recessionary pressures may make the target customers more price sensitive than when they had a higher margin of disposable income. Perhaps a new competitor has grown with aggressive marketing that needs a rapid response.

What should not be forgotten is what was good and bad about the previous promotional campaign. What can they learn from to improve the present promotion?

This book will take you through a detailed exploration of how best we can embed the good discipline that effective project management can engender into its marketing operations.

SYNERGIES BETWEEN MARKETING AND PROJECT MANAGEMENT

Project management techniques have relevance to all aspects of marketing. For example,

- market research and internal audits give us information to help in deciding what project is most viable,
- planning tools help decide the overall approach we will take,
- the project implementation is through the marketing mix,
- feedback, control and evaluation are common to both.

This text looks at the use of project management techniques as a continuing framework within which the collection and processing of information, risk assessment, project evaluation and decision making are done, through to planning, analysis, implementation and control.

The four sections are shown below with their syllabus weighting. Within each of these sections, the content is broken down into a series of chapters that follow the sequence of marketing project life cycles.

Links to the syllabus are clearly indicated as syllabus references and learning outcomes. For each section, comments of the senior examiner are included to enhance understanding.

Case studies are used throughout to show real-life examples. Each complete section has its own bibliography to assist you in further exploring those materials.

SUMMARY

Although quite a lot of the content is new, the fundamental underlying concepts and principles of marketing management remain intact with adaptation where necessary. That adaptation is to align these fundamentals with the fundamentals that exist within other management disciplines; in this instance, project management.

The inextricable link between the bases of everyday marketing management and practice with the core frameworks and models of sound project management are manipulated and extrapolated within this unit. There is no desire to reconstitute any theory or practice, but rather to encourage the marriage of best practice from a multidisciplinary appreciation.

The unit aims to:

- Encourage a deep and rigorous approach to collecting and analysing information and data from disparate secondary sources.

- Promote the recognition that information gaps exist and should be bridged by some form of primary research undertaking in order to fully build and present justified business cases.

- Enhance organisational orientation, whereby identifying, analysing, managing and mitigating risk becomes embedded in all elements of the marketing management process.

- Apply and align the core concepts of marketing management with project management to a variety of organisational marketing problems.

KEY LEARNING OUTCOMES

The syllabus document gives details of the unit introduction, aims and objectives, learning outcomes and other guidance. The key learning outcomes that students should be able to achieve include:

- Identifying the organisation's information needs, scope of research projects and resource capability to underpin the development of a business case to support marketing projects.

- Developing an effective business case, complete with justifications, financial assessments and consideration of the organisation's resource capacity and capability to deliver.

- Undertaking a risk assessment programme with suggestions on how to mitigate for risks facing the organisation and the achievement of its business and marketing objectives.

- Designing, developing and planning significant marketing programmes, using project management tools and techniques designed to deliver marketing projects effectively, in terms of quality, resource and delivery.

- Integrating a range of marketing tools and techniques to support the development and implementation of a range of marketing projects.

- Monitoring and measuring the effectiveness and outcomes of marketing projects through the end-to-end project process.

The Marketing Planning Process unit will instil the necessary rigour required to systematically examine business environments via the use of marketing audit tools. This unit will drill down and focus that approach to situation-specific contexts. Unit 2, Delivering Customer Value Through Marketing, will introduce the students to core concepts that lend themselves to project management initiatives around product portfolios, marketing channels, communications and service expectation, and these will be fully explored via assessment diets. Furthermore, the Managing Marketing unit will support the necessary underlying control frameworks that are also imperative throughout the project management process.

ASSESSMENT

The assessment for this unit is a work-based assessment, which requires the students to apply the learning they have undertaken in an integrated way and bring together various aspects of their studies to solve organisational problems or to develop new organisational initiatives. The assessment will expect students to use either their own organisation or one they know well as a starting point.

The assessment is aligned to the CIM assessment criteria and is based on the magic formula that is applied on the basis of:

Concept (30%)
Application (30%)
Evaluation (30%)
Presentation (10%)

Frank McKee
Senior CIM Examiner – Project Management in Marketing
2009–2010

About the Authors

Frank McKee is a freelance marketing practitioner with over 20 years experience as a sales and marketing consultant and tutor. He has written, delivered and assessed courses, seminars and workshops for many institutions such as Belfast Metropolitan College; Queen's University Belfast and the Open University. Frank is also a visiting tutor at Henley Management College on the International Executive MBA programme. In addition to his role as a Senior Examiner for the Chartered Institute of Marketing, he is also a Subject Examiner for a number of professional and academic awarding bodies.

Elwyn Cox gained extensive business experience in both project management and business consultancy before moving full-time into education. As a Senior Marketing Lecturer at the University of Winchester he also has a specific interest in sports marketing, presenting on this to the 2008 CIM conference. He was involved in the syllabus review idea generating workshops. He passed his Diploma in Marketing in 1972 – a fact that frightens him.

Matthew Housden is a Principal Lecturer in Marketing, University of Greenwich Business School; Tutor and Senior Consultant at the IDM; full member of the Market Research Society and ESOMAR; and member of CIM.

Lynn Parkinson is a previous CIM Senior Examiner for the Advanced Certificate in Professional Sales and the Advanced Certificate in Key Account Management, and a highly experienced marketing lecturer and trainer.

Using Marketing Information to Develop a Justified Case for Marketing Projects (Weighting 15%)

Shown below are the syllabus references and learning outcomes for this section. It is the first of the four that comprise the complete unit. The chapters that make up the section are also shown. This will be the same for all four sections to assist the student in understanding how individual themes build into the completed text and what the progression is from one to the next.

SYLLABUS REFERENCES

1.1 Critically assess the scope and type of marketing information required to develop effective business cases using both primary and secondary data

1.2 Critically assess how organisations determine their marketing information requirements and the key elements of user specifications for the purposes of building a case

1.3 Critically assess the scope, structure and characteristics of MIS and MkIS as marketing management support systems and evaluate their importance to business cases for marketing projects

1.4 Develop a research brief to meet the requirements of an individually specific case for marketing

1.5 Critically evaluate a full research proposal to fulfil the brief supporting the information needs of the case and make recommendations for improvement

1.6 Identify and evaluate the most effective methods for presenting marketing information and making specific marketing recommendations relating to product/service development and implementation as part of the case

Chapter 1 – Marketing Information for Business Cases
Chapter 2 – Marketing Information Systems
Chapter 3 – Research Briefs and Proposals
Chapter 4 – Presentation of Findings
Senior Examiner's Comments
Bibliography

LEARNING OUTCOMES

Identify the organisation's information needs, scope of research projects and resource capability to underpin the development of a business case to support marketing projects.

LEARNING OBJECTIVES

By the end of this section, you will be able to:

- Assess the scope and type of marketing information requirements
- Assess the structure and characteristics of marketing information systems
- Understand the relationship between brief and proposal
- Understand how to select from, and use, a range of primary research tools
- Select and adapt different report and presentation techniques

CHAPTER 1

Marketing Information for Business Cases

Note: those who have started at this point are strongly recommended to go back and carefully read the Foreword. It explains not just the idea behind this new unit, but how the book is structured, central themes and how to get the most out of it.

INTRODUCTION

Peter Chisnall in his 2004 book *Marketing Research* calls information the raw material of management. Without information we cannot make informed decisions. There will always be risk attached to business decisions, but good information will help us measure, manage and assess the degree of risk involved in making business and marketing decisions.

DEFINING THE ISSUES OR PROBLEM

Defining the problem, despite appearances, is not easy. Problems can generally be solved in many ways. The problem definition needs to reflect the organisation's resources, or be expressed in a way that clearly identifies the opportunity that is being looked at.

Sometimes, a view of the problem for a pressured executive may not actually be the real issue. The research company that is asked to review marketing communications activity may find that there are particular political issues with the current agency or that the brand is poorly managed or that the pricing strategy is wrong. Very often we have to carry out informal or exploratory research to identify and define the research question we are trying to answer.

Poorly researched questions or problem definitions can lead to expensive and unnecessary work being carried out.

Clearly then, being able to define a problem and set objectives in an appropriate way is very important.

Often managers appear to want the answer to the meaning of life by 5.00 p.m. Understanding the business so as to be able to isolate and define a problem is a skill that comes with experience. For example, the ill-informed manager may say set an objective to determine 'why are our sales falling?', while the experienced manager might say 'what are the perceptions of our service standards against our key competitors?' He has already limited the research to a narrow problem area and researchers have a much clearer idea of the purpose to which the research will be put. It may be that the researcher has to carry out this refining and defining process, but it can be helped by good communication and understanding at this stage.

CARRY OUT EXPLORATORY RESEARCH

This stage, as outlined above, is designed to clarify the research problem. It is largely informal and may involve a range of techniques. It should involve discussions with those who are involved with the problem and its solution. It may involve a review of the trade press and simple scanning of internal documents and resources. The aim is to inform the process and to become 'immersed' in the problem and its potential solutions.

Even at this stage, the researcher may be thinking ahead about methods that could be used to deliver the information required. The key thing is to uncover the real purpose of the research and, possibly, the constraints in terms of time and budget that may affect the process.

We also need, at this stage, to think about the value of the research. There is little point in spending more on research than will be gained by making the right decision as a result of it – it has to be cost-effective. Research cannot eliminate risk entirely, but tries to reduce it to acceptable levels within identifiable margins of error. An understanding of the commercial constraints of carrying out research may be gained through intuition or experience, but it can also be worked out more scientifically.

If research is required to justify packaging redesign, then we can estimate the improved sales of such a move and offset the cost of research against this. This objective-and-task approach to setting research budgets is the best way of managing research budgets. However, it is not always possible to carry out this process accurately.

If the cost of a research project to decide between two product flavours was £25,000, and the research-based launch generated incremental profits of £40,000, then clearly the research is worthwhile. It should always be possible to estimate the likely impact on a project, if it is done with or without research and this can help in determining whether the research should be done (in the first place) and the extent of what research is needed.

PREVIOUS RESEARCH

As part of this process, previously carried out research should be reviewed to see if the problem has been dealt with elsewhere. It may be that the solution lies in work that has been done in other departments. For example, work to improve the navigation of the website may have been done in the IT department. Access to previously commissioned work may be through the Intranet or the company library. Or it may be that individual managers have commissioned research which has not been distributed widely through the organisations.

INTERNAL RESEARCH

Internal research will involve the use of the MkIS (Marketing Information System – a subset of Management Information System) and the database. It may be that the problem, as we said, can be solved at this stage. Normally it is worth spending time now on internal records to either solve the problem or at least help to define it.

For example, a problem that involves finding out the average age of a company's existing customers may be solved through a simple interrogation of the customer database.

REDEFINE THE PROBLEM

The output of this stage is a clear statement of the research problem that is agreed by all parties. After this, a brief can be written based on the work to date.

DESK RESEARCH

Desk or secondary research is information that has already been gathered for some other purpose. It may be held within the organisation or by other organisations. It is called desk research because it is usually accessible from a desk via the Intranet or online or in hard copy. This is dealt with in detail in the next section. In the research plan, desk research is carried out before primary research. This is because it is generally cheaper. It may solve the problem without any need for expensive primary work.

FIELD RESEARCH

Field or primary research is research carried out to meet a specific objective. It is something new that adds to the body of world research. Primary research is the common currency of marketing research. It is what most of us have come across either through telephone research, or face-to-face interviews or increasingly through online research.

Primary research may be based on observation and may be qualitative or quantitative.

Observation research is data gathered by observing behaviour. No questions are asked of participants, whereas much research is based upon structured questionnaires designed to give a consistent quality of response to a range of predetermined questions as expanded upon below.

The Marketing Research Society (MRS) defines observational research as 'A non-verbal means of obtaining primary data as an alternative or complement to questioning.'

QUALITATIVE RESEARCH

Qualitative research describes research that cannot be quantified or subjected to quantitative analysis. It typically uses small sample sizes and is designed to produce a depth of understanding, context and insight. It helps to uncover the motivation behind the behaviour rather than to identify the behaviour itself. It seeks to get under the skin of respondents, uncovering their deeper feelings. It is essentially subjective but it is a highly developed and important research methodology.

MRS defines qualitative research as 'A body of research techniques that seeks insights through loosely structured, mainly verbal data rather than measurements. Analysis is interpretative, subjective, impressionistic and diagnostic.'

QUANTITATIVE RESEARCH

Quantitative is the opposite of qualitative in that it is statistically verifiable. It provides answers to the questions 'who' and 'how many' rather than the depth of insight as to why. It uses a structured approach to problem-solving using a sample of the population to make statistically based assumptions about the behaviour of the population as a whole.

MRS defines quantitative research as 'Research that seeks to make measurements as distinct from qualitative research.'

Note that the distinction between qualitative and quantitative can sometimes become blurred – a scaled response to a question can be measured depending on number of occurrences within the points along the scale. However, the response to the questions may indicate a depth of feeling. Often a more open-ended supplementary question is specifically created to get a deeper level of quantitative analysis.

FIELDWORK

Fieldwork is the generic term given to the collection of primary data. It may cover the collection of observational, quantitative and qualitative data. The administration of a major quantitative study may involve serious logistical considerations whilst qualitative work may involve highly qualified and skilled researchers. The management of fieldwork is often given to specialist field managers or fieldwork agencies. The process is very important as the failure to adhere to methodology at this stage may compromise the entire project.

DATA INPUT, CODING AND EDITING

Data that is gathered from respondents must be recorded and edited to produce a data set that is capable of being analysed. In qualitative work, this may mean producing a transcript of the interview. In quantitative work, it means creating a data set that the computer can work with.

All potential responses must be given a different code to enable analysis. Data is checked for completeness and consistency, and if there are significant problems the respondent may be called back to check details. Often today, data is input straight into the computer via systems known as CATI (computer-assisted telephone interviewing), CAPI (computer-assisted personal interviewing) and CAWI (computer-assisted web interviewing) www.marketresearchworld.net.

Note that some sources may use the phrase computer-aided rather than computer-assisted.

DATA ANALYSIS

Data is analysed using computers to produce a range of results, but while computers may do the calculations it is people that have to interpret the potential impact of those results and make decisions accordingly. Data is a series of facts, but it is finding a use for appropriate data that changes it to information. The right questions need to be asked.

For example, 'half past three this afternoon' makes no sense until it is framed as a response to the question 'what time is the next bus to the city centre'?

RESULTS, FINDINGS AND RECOMMENDATIONS

A marketing decision should result from the results of the research. Results should be presented clearly in a way that focuses on the problem to be solved. It is easy with today's statistical packages to produce hundreds of tables to a high degree of statistical sophistication. Results must be presented in a way that is accessible to the audience and that presents clearly the solution to the problem posed.

We live in the knowledge age where so much can be found at the click of a mouse button. There is a danger of information overload that hides the reason why a question was posed in the first place.

REPORT OR PRESENTATION

Presentation of the results will usually be in the form of a written report and often this is supported by an oral presentation. The data will need to be presented, but this should be in the appendices. The body of the report remains solutions-focused.

DECISION

The output should be marketing decisions that are made at reduced risk and a feedback loop should exist to the business situation. Feedback should continue to monitor the situation post-implementation, so that fine-tuning can be made.

SUMMARY

We looked at the fact that the efficient solution of problems through research means that we should start with the cheapest sources of information, i.e. secondary or desk research.

If this does not produce the required information, then we move to primary work.

We outlined the different types of marketing research and looked at qualitative and quantitative work.

We saw that qualitative work should precede and inform the development of quantitative methodology.

We looked at the difference between qualitative and quantitative work.

CHAPTER 2

Marketing Information Systems

INTRODUCTION

Without pertinent, reliable, accurate and timely information, decision making would be impossible. Management decisions would be made in a vacuum. Without information and intelligent analysis of the data, the organisation is disconnected from its markets, suppliers, people, customers and future.

Some markets change quickly, others evolve, but they always change. As Hugh Davidson (1997) says, 'tomorrow's standards are always higher'. The information strategy of the organisation must be set up to ensure that these changes can be anticipated, monitored and acted upon. Risk can never be eliminated from business decision making. The key thing is to manage and, where possible, reduce the risk to which the organisation is subject to acceptable levels relative to the required return on shareholders' investments.

Integrated information is critical to effective decision making. Marketing information sources can be thought of as separate jigsaw pieces; only when

CASE EXAMPLE – Wal-Mart knows its business

Hurricane Frances was on its way, barrelling across the Caribbean, threatening a direct hit on Florida's Atlantic coast. Residents made for higher ground, but far away, in Bentonville, Arkansas, executives at Wal-Mart Stores decided that the situation offered a great opportunity for one of their newest data-driven weapons, something that the company calls predictive technology.

A week ahead of the storm's landfall, Linda M. Dillman, Wal-Mart's chief information officer pressed her staff to come up with forecasts based on what had happened when Hurricane Charley struck several weeks earlier. Backed by the trillions of bytes' worth of shopper history that is stored in Wal-Mart's computer network, she felt that the company could 'start predicting what's going to happen, instead of waiting for it to happen', as she put it. The experts mined the data and found that the stores would indeed need certain products – and not just the usual flashlights. 'We didn't know in the past that strawberry Pop-Tarts increased in sales, like seven times their normal sales rate, ahead of a hurricane', Ms. Dillman said in a recent interview, 'and the pre-hurricane top-selling item was beer'.

Thanks to those insights, trucks filled with toaster pastries and six-packs were soon speeding down Interstate 95 towards Wal-Mart in the path of Frances. Most of the products that were stocked for the storm sold quickly, the company said. Such knowledge, Wal-Mart has learned, is not only power. It is profit, too.

Plenty of retailers collect data about their stores and their shoppers, and many use the information to try to improve sales. Target Stores, for example, introduced a branded Visa card in 2001 and has used it, along with an arsenal of gadgetry, to gather data ever since. But Wal-Mart amasses more data about the products it sells and its shoppers' buying habits than anyone else, so much so that some privacy advocates worry about potential for abuse.

With 3600 stores in the United States and roughly 100 million customers walking through the doors each week, Wal-Mart has access to information about a broad slice of America – from individual Social Security and driver's license numbers to geographic proclivities for Mallomars, or lipsticks or jugs of antifreeze. The data are gathered item by item at the checkout aisle, then recorded, mapped and updated by store, by state and by region.

By its own count, Wal-Mart has 460 terabytes of data stored on Teradata mainframes, made by NCR, at its Bentonville headquarters. To put that in perspective, the Internet has less than half as much data according to experts. Information about products, and often about customers, is most often obtained at checkout scanners. Wireless handheld units, operated by clerks and managers, gather more inventory data. In most cases, such detail is stored for indefinite lengths of time. Sometimes it is divided into categories or mapped across computer models, and it is increasingly being used to answer discount retailing's rabbinical questions, like how many cashiers are needed during certain hours at a particular store.

All of the data are precious to Wal-Mart. The information forms the basis of the sales meetings the company holds every Saturday, and it is shot across desktops throughout its headquarters and into the places where it does business around the world. Wal-Mart shares some information with its suppliers – a company like Kraft, for example, can tap into a private extranet called Retail Link to see how well its products are selling.

Source: New York Times, November 2004.

they are connected does the whole picture become clear. Taking decisions by looking at each of the pieces individually is not only inefficient, but is also likely to result in wrong assumptions and decisions being made (Wilson, 2006).

What we see here is that advantage in the marketplace does not simply come from carrying out research; it is about identifying, collating, understanding, analysing and acting upon the many diverse sources of knowledge within an organisation. Wal-Mart is one organisation that manages this very well.

The aim of knowledge management is to integrate systems and individuals to enable and encourage knowledge transfer between employees and other stakeholders. For example, knowledge management systems may work between retailers and their suppliers to ensure 'just-in-time' delivery of new stock, to plan and implement sales-promotion campaigns and to jointly manage the marketing research that underpins new product development.

ACTIVITY 2.1

You are the research-and-insight manager for a large food manufacturer. Outline the sources of knowledge that might feed a knowledge management system.

MARKETING MANAGEMENT SUPPORT SYSTEMS – THE MARKETING INFORMATION SYSTEM (MKIS)

The MkIS is a term that has largely fallen out of favour in the marketing world. It has been replaced by a whole tranche of new descriptors, the most common amongst these being CRM systems and database marketing. What we are looking at in this section is the range of tools that exists to help the marketing manager handle the vast amount of information that he or she has access to today.

The MkIS is the system that organisations use to put information at the heart of the decision-making process.

The MkIS defined by Kotler 'consists of people, equipment and procedures to gather, sort, analyse, evaluate and distribute timely and accurate information to marketing decision makers' (Kotler *et al.*, 2007).

The typical MkIS consists of four elements:

1. The marketing research system – This is the backbone of the marketing information system. However, the MkIS also contains other elements. These are as follows:

2. The marketing intelligence system – This refers to the published data existing in the marketplace. It may include published research reports, government statistics or the national or trade press. We will look at this in detail when we examine secondary research.

3. The decision-support system – This contains the tools needed to make sense of data; it may include statistical packages and the intranet, with a range of tools and information designed to help marketers make decisions.

4. Internal records – These include sales records, accounts records, details on past communications and the results of previously commissioned marketing research.

These last elements are often now consolidated within the marketing database. Let us look at the two mainstays of the MkIS in turn, starting with marketing research.

THE DATABASE

The other elements of the MkIS are often incorporated within the marketing database. Alan Wilson (2006) defines the marketing database as: 'A manual or computerised source of data relevant to marketing decision-making about an organisation's customers'.

There are a few things about this definition that need to be explained.

A database does not have to be computer-based. It can be kept on hard copy. However, access to database technology is very easy and cheap. Even the cheapest and simplest software is capable of storing a significant number of records. Microsoft Access is perfectly serviceable for many businesses.

While the definition limits itself to 'customers', other definitions spell out the fact that the database will collect data about past and potential customers as well as current customers. De Tienne and Thompson use the following definition of database marketing:

The process of systematically collecting in electronic or optical form data about past, current and/or potential customers, maintaining the integrity of the data by continually monitoring customer purchases and/or by inquiring about changing status and using the data to formulate marketing strategy and foster personalised relationships with customers (De Tienne and Thompson, 1996).

The IDM (Institute of Direct Marketing) defines the marketing database as 'a comprehensive collection of inter-related customer and/or prospect data that allows the timely accurate retrieval, use or manipulation of that data to support the marketing objectives of the enterprise' (cited in Downer, 2002).

Wilson says that the database differs from an accounting system in that the data must be relevant to marketing decision making. This is a subtle but important difference. Clearly, the accounting system may reveal very interesting information to the marketer. It may contain details of what the customer has bought and when, and the frequency of purchase. We will see later that this information is important to successful database marketing. However, it is important that the data fed into the marketing database is relevant to marketing decisions now and in the future. It costs money to store and process data, and in this information age it is easy to have too much data.

INFORMATION AND THE SCOPE OF MARKETING RESEARCH

So what is marketing information used for? The clue is in the definitions in the section above. But let us try and be more specific.

ACTIVITY 2.2

Think about a marketing project process. How does marketing information help this process? Write as many things as you can. Use your textbooks when you run out of ideas.

DATA PROTECTION AND FREEDOM OF INFORMATION

The United Kingdom has had data protection legislation since 1984. The current Data Protection Act that was passed in 1998 and came into force in 2000 was introduced in response to the 1995 European Union Directive on Data Protection. The Act regulates 'processing' of data; this covers data on any living person, and there are separate rules for sensitive data, for example, health, sexuality, religion, disabilities and so on. If you collect data on Halal meals, then your data falls in this separate, more sensitive category. The Freedom of Information Act (2000) came into force on 1 January, 2005. The Act regulates access to information held by public authorities.

The guiding principles of transparency and consent in the Data Protection Act are most relevant for marketing research professionals. Individuals must have a clear understanding of why their data is being captured and what it will be used for, and they must consent to its use and be given the opportunity to opt out of any later use of this data.

Opt-out is the standard at the moment. However, this is changing, and the latest rules seem to be asking people to actively 'opt in' to future use of their data (an extension of the principle of permission marketing). This is very likely to become the standard, and it is good practice now to ask individuals to actively opt in to the future use of their data.

USING THE DATABASE TO PROFILE YOUR CUSTOMERS

Profiling is something that the database allows us to do quite easily. Because of the range of information that we capture on our customers, we can create quite sophisticated profiles of our customers. By linking our database to services like Mosaic and Acxiom's products, we can extend this profile significantly. For example, a Mosaic code based on a customer's postcode will also unlock information collected by BMRB (British Market Research Bureau) through a service called the Target Group Index (TGI) (see below). This means that we can effectively link our base with TGI data on the basis of over 25,000 customer interviews.

Simple profiling might be used to identify the best-value customers according to certain demographic or lifestyle indicators. This would be based on the value of past purchases, how often they purchased and when they last purchased. This is known as recency, frequency and value analysis or RFV analysis. You may also see it written as FRAC (frequency, recency, amount and category) analysis. By matching this to other data, for example, income, family status and postcode, we can identify similar people in the market who do not transact with us and target them for acquisition.

Of course, the process of identifying these top customers allows us to begin the process of retaining them. It is believed that it costs between 3 and 30 times more to acquire a customer than it does to retain a customer.

Reichheld's book *The Loyalty Effect* goes into this in far more detail (Reichheld, 2001).

Academic research shows that the use of modelling and profiling via the database is a far more reliable and profitable approach to decision making in marketing.

CASE EXAMPLE – The financial services sector

The financial services sector is a heavy user of database analysis. Amongst others, a major bank has used their database in the following ways:

1. To manage the branch network
   a. Identifying the most profitable branches
   b. Staff appraisal, monitoring, reward and recognition
   c. To identify staff training needs
   d. To manage branch location
2. To acquire new customers
   a. Through profiling of good, existing customers and using this
   b. To plan for the acquisition of new customers
3. To increase profitability of existing customers
   a. Reducing the cost of marketing
   b. Improved targeting
   c. Personalizing marketing communications
   d. Reduce attrition
4. Developing new products
5. Developing new market segments

ACTIVITY 2.3

Create a profile of your internal or external customer base using whatever data and key information is held within your organisational systems.

- What are their core characteristics?
- What defines similar groupings?
- How would you translate behaviour patterns?

SUMMARY

We looked at the MkIS as the mechanism for delivering this information and in detail explored marketing research and the database as the key components of this system. The database is defined as: 'A manual or computerised source of data relevant to marketing decision-making about an organisation's customers' (Wilson, 2006).

CHAPTER 3

Research Briefs and Proposals

INTRODUCTION

We now move on to the discipline of marketing research. In this chapter, we explore the process of planning research and briefing researchers to carry out the process. This will be an important part of your course. The senior examiner in a recent briefing to tutors told them to focus on the process of developing research briefs, responding to those briefs through the presentation of the proposal and then presenting the final report.

This activity represents the day-to-day management of the research function in business and you may expect it to form a relative part of your assessment in this unit.

The brief is very important. Even if the research is to be carried out in-house, a briefing document is required. It provides a fixed reference that all parties involved should sign off.

For the commissioner of the research, it provides 'bulletproof' evidence that certain dates or budgets were agreed on. In complex research studies, it keeps all parties on track and can help the process of project management.

ACTIVITY 3.1

You are the marketing manager for a major soft drinks producer. Sales have stagnated in the over 50's segment and you have been asked to look at the development of a new drink to target the older market. What core information would you need to be establishing to enable you to undertake such a project?

THE MARKETING RESEARCH BRIEF

We will now look more in detail at the marketing research brief. The briefing document is perhaps the most important stage of the research process. As the old aphorism states, 'be careful what you ask for, you may get it'. A tight brief is vital to the management of the marketing research process. It provides a focus for discussion and a guiding hand through the project.

Many companies see the briefing process as part of an almost gladiatorial trial of strength where a brief is issued, limited information is given, and the resulting proposals are torn to bits in the arena of the pitch. The justification is that ideas are tested in the heat of the moment and that if an agency cannot justify an approach under fire, they are unlikely to be effective. The lack of detail is seen as allowing the agency to interpret and explore ideas. Some research briefs are given on one side of a page of A4. This may be sufficient, but is almost certainly inadequate for complex multifaceted research tasks.

Equally, some companies go the other way, even specifying the colour and weight of paper for the final presentation. This may be overkill.

On the other side, some agencies receive a brief as Drayton Bird (2007) says, 'rather like a baby bird waiting to be fed by its mother, passively, humbly and gratefully'. Both approaches are wrong. The best marketing solutions come through co-operation and active involvement.

Agencies need the right information in order to be able to produce a suitable proposal. If there are issues over confidentiality, then confidentiality agreements can be signed before the brief is issued. Members of the MRS are obliged to comply with the code of conduct that ensures client confidentiality. However, the agency needs the tools to do the job – in this case, information. The development of the brief should be a team activity. The structure is outlined below:

Identification details – These should include the title, date, contact names and details.

Current business position – This should detail the nature and scope of the business, key markets served, key competitors and future direction.

Marketing and business objectives – Should be laid down and distinguished between.

Research objectives – Will almost certainly differ from marketing objectives but are informed by them. For example, the marketing objectives may be to enter a new market while the research objectives may be to identify the product attributes that appeal most to potential customers.

How the results will be used – The overall purpose and context for the research needs to be specified. How will the research be used and what other decisions might it inform in the future?

Outline methodology – This is a difficult area but in discussing the problem, research methods may have been discussed. Certainly, where there is expertise in the briefing team, the research methodology may have been discussed in detail. There is no danger in allowing the proposing agency to have access to these views. Certainly, the brief should include details on whether a qualitative or quantitative approach is required. Also, outline question areas could be given.

Sample details – The details of the group of interest should be indicated. If the sample is to include businesses over a certain size, then the agency should be told to avoid wasting their time.

Previous research – Previously commissioned work that is relevant to the current study may be outlined or made available to the agency pitching for the business.

Timings – It is important that a detailed timetable of activity is included. This should cover time for questions, and details of the formal date and time for the presentation to take place if this is required.

Budget – A tricky area, but generally it is advisable to give some indication of the budget that is available for the project.

Deliverables – How will the results be presented and when? Will there be a formal debriefing presentation? How many copies of reports will be needed?

Terms and conditions – These can include confidentiality, payment terms and penalty clauses amongst others.

Key personnel names – And details of all key staff involved in the project.

(*Note*: Following is an illustrative cut-down brief presented to ensure client confidentiality.)

Purpose of the research – to establish usage and attitudes to the consumption of ambient ready meals in the five EU markets (specified elsewhere).

Background to the company
Description of the company: ownership, turnover, brands, ambient ready meal (ARM) brands.
   Market size and market share data, trends, volume and values, competition

Background to the problem
Falling retail share, seek to stabilise market share through refined mix

Research objectives

- Why are ARMs bought?
- When are they used?
- Who prepares them?
- On what occasions are they used?
- Perception of quality relative to other RM (ready meal) categories
- Perception of quality relative to competitors
- Attitudes to price
- Attitudes to advertising

Methods

1. Qualitative analysis
      Focus groups in key target audiences

2. Quantitative analysis
   Around 1500 housewives in each market, representative of
   households, quota sample
   Question areas built out of the qualitative study
   Brands bought, brands recognised, consumption occasion,
   attitudes to ARMs and other RM categories
   Client input requested on this aspect of research, design and
   implementation

Timing
Proposal: 2 April; Presentation: week commencing 12 April; Commission:
4 May; Report: early July

Budget
In the region of £25,000

Report to
Brand manager, Marketing research manager, Marketing director

THE PROPOSAL

The proposal should be presented in a written format and on time. A formal presentation may accompany the proposal. The proposal itself should
be seen before any formal face-to-face presentation in order for it to be
assessed and questions framed. These questions may be sent to the agency
before the formal meeting.

Proposals may form the final contract for a project and as such can
include contract details and terms and conditions as an appendix. It is also
a marketing tool for the research agency, so the use of client testimonials
and relevant past contracts is normal. It is fundamental that presentation,
spelling and grammar should be faultless.

Identification data

- Key contact details, title and date.
- Situation analysis
- An outline of the current business position

Research objectives

- A clear statement of the purposes of the research
- Methodology and rationale

Crouch and Housden (2003) suggest that the following questions should be
answered:

1. Why use the sample selection procedure indicated?
2. Why use the size of sample indicated?

3. Why the personal interview technique rather than group discussion?
4. Why a 20-minute questionnaire and not a 30-minute questionnaire?
5. Why are open-ended questions requiring expensive coding and analysis being included in a large-scale quantitative survey?
6. Why is a written report or verbal presentation included, or why not?
7. Why the timetable indicated?
8. Why is the cost indicated?

Sample
A precise definition of the sample to be selected and a justification of this.

Fieldwork
What data-collection methods are proposed?

Questionnaire or topic guide
It is unreasonable to expect a final questionnaire but an indication of what the agency expects to see in the questionnaire should be provided.

Data handling and processing
How will data be captured, edited, coded and analysed? What tables will be provided? How will the data be presented?

Reporting
What is included in the scope of the report?

Timetable
A full detailed timetable of research activity and key milestones.

Costs
What is included? Is VAT included? How long is the quote valid? Terms of business and payment schedule.

Curriculum Vitae (CVs) of key staff
Are the people who are presenting, the people you will be dealing with? What is their experience? What professional memberships do they have?

Supporting evidence
Is the agency a member of professional bodies? Are references provided?

Contract details
The proposal will generally form the contract on acceptance.

IN-HOUSE OR OUT-OF-HOUSE

Whether to carry out all or some of the tasks using in-house resources and expertise, rather than third-party agencies, will need to be considered. Shown below is a set of variables that would need evaluating fully before the decision could be made.

In-house has a range of advantages:

- Control of the research process rests with those who commissioned the work.
- Awareness of the market or sector dynamics.
- Knowledge of both methodology and results resides within the organisation of the cumulative knowledge.
- Costs – it may be cheaper to manage the tasks in-house.
- Timing – it may be quicker to produce results.

Disadvantages may include:

- Lack of skills or methodological expertise.
- Inability to provide true national or international coverage (applies to smaller businesses in particular).
- Bias in terms of interpreting the result from a predetermined point of view – an agency should be neutral.

Advantages of using an agency include:

- Tighter cost control may be possible.
- Penalty clauses in contracts can protect the commissioning party.
- MRS code of conduct or other industry quality-control standards will ensure the integrity of data.
- There is no political element to the research.

Disadvantages:

- Conflict of interest with other clients.
- Lack of industry expertise.
- Allocation of junior staff to smaller projects.

ACTIVITY 3.2

Based on Activity 3.1, develop an in-house proposal to fit the in-house brief.

SUMMARY

We looked at the briefing process and looked at each stage in turn. We saw that the brief was an important document and that the proposal that answers or accompanies it, ultimately, will become the template for the research programme.

We looked at the process of producing a proposal and the pros and cons of in-house versus out-of-house resources and expertise.

CHAPTER 4

Presentation of Findings

INTRODUCTION

The final report is perhaps the most important part of the research process. In practice, this is a very stressful time. Not only are decisions to be made as to where the work will be allocated, but for individuals, it is the chance to impress senior colleagues and enhance their reputation.

The ability to present data in the most appropriate and accessible way, whilst ensuring that the research problem is effectively dealt with, is a highly developed skill.

The results are generally presented in written format and this may or may not be supported by an oral presentation supported by slides.

Wilson suggests a six-point approach to the presentation of research that focuses on the audience's needs.

1. Respect their importance.
2. What do they need from the report?
3. How does your report meet this need?
4. Underpin the key information with evidence.
5. Remind them of the key points of the report.
6. Make recommendations as to action.

THE WRITTEN REPORT

The structure of a written report is standard and this helps considerably with the process of producing the document. Before producing the report, it helps to consider the objectives of the study again and the nature of the audience who will read and use the report.

What are the key points that the audience is interested in? What are the key constraints on marketing decisions recommended in the report? What is the business position and are the resource implications of decisions adequately considered?

TITLE PAGE

This should contain the title of the report, the author, the organisation and the date of presentation.

CONTENTS PAGE

This should contain full details of sections, subsections and page numbers, and include lists of tables and figures. It should make the report navigable. If presenting on the Web, the use of hyperlinks that take the browser to the relevant section can be considered.

THE EXECUTIVE SUMMARY

This should be a short summary of the report and its recommendations. Many say that it should be a one- or two-page summary, or a maximum of two pages. There are no hard and fast rules. The summary needs to do the job of summarising a report, but it also needs to be clear and accessible to readers.

Production of the executive summary is a tough job. As Churchill said, 'Sorry, for such a long letter. I didn't have time to write a short one'. It is hard to condense the report into a one- or two-page summary. It is also the section of the report that will be read by senior managers and so it is worth putting time and effort into its production.

The executive summary should be written after the rest of the report has been completed, but should be positioned at the start of the report. Some people feel that it should follow the contents page and some feel that it should precede it. Some companies produce a separate summary of the work and this can be useful for a wider and more efficient distribution of the key findings of the report. In business, different organisations will have their preferred structure and layout – a house style.

Generally, companies that are producing a large number of reports will include the format of the report in their identity guidelines or will have formal guidelines elsewhere that should be followed. The font size and appearance must do justice to your work and the sequencing of the report with its headers and subheaders should make the report more accessible. A style guide might also be used to help with language, grammar and even brand messages through the report.

If you are unsure of your use of English, then it is always best to get somebody professional to proofread your work for spelling, grammar and punctuation. Remember that proofreading is different from reading the report through.

Each word and sentence needs to be considered individually as well as in connection with the rest of the report.

INTRODUCTION

The introduction should outline the key objectives of the research, the reasons why the research has been carried out and the constraints that the researchers are working to. It may include profiles and key responsibilities of the researchers.

SITUATION ANALYSIS AND PROBLEM DEFINITION

This section outlines the background to the problem and reviews business and marketing objectives. It drills down into the problem's definition and the detailed objectives for the research programme, and reprises the sections of the brief and proposal.

RESEARCH METHODOLOGY AND LIMITATIONS

This section outlines the detailed methodology for the study. It should cover the research method; the data-capture mechanism, the topic, discussion guide or questionnaire, the definition of the population of interest, the sampling approach and the method of data analysis.

This section should not be too long. Details should be put into the appendices. It should cover potential sources of error, including sample size.

FINDINGS AND ANALYSIS

The main body of the report looks at the findings relevant to the objectives. It should be constructed to present a solution to the problem, not on a question-by-question basis. The research data should present data to support a line of argument and the focus should be on analysis and insight. Tables or quotes from respondents can support key ideas. It may include tables and graphics, and should be linked by a narrative.

Remember that your audience is in solutions to the problem far more than a restating of the background – get the balance the right way around.

CONCLUSIONS AND RECOMMENDATIONS

This section brings the report to a close. It should present a summary of key findings and recommendations for marketing decisions and future research.

APPENDICES

They should include all supporting data. This is material that is relevant to the research, but that would be too detailed for the main report. Typically, it will hold all tables, questionnaires, discussion guides and secondary data and it may well be that the appendices are longer than the main report.

THE ORAL PRESENTATION

The process of delivering an oral presentation may be daunting, but prior preparation and practice should mean that it does not have to be too nerve-wracking. In many cases, nerves are a good sign that this matters.

The oral presentation may involve a number of people and a range of audio and visual equipment. The technology is always a problem and it is reassuring to have a backup. If there is a chance to have a trial run using the equipment and setting that the actual presentation will take place in, that opportunity should be taken. Familiarity will help engender confidence.

The key thing in preparing a presentation is that it is not simply a regurgitation of the written report. The presentation, of course, draws on the same data and makes the same conclusions but the findings can be presented in a much livelier and, maybe, accessible and memorable way.

USE OF GRAPHICS

Tables and graphs will enliven reports and presentations, but with the range of technology available, overkill is possible.

TABLES

Tables should be presented with the title and a number. The tables should be labelled with base numbers; that is, the figures for the sample and sub-samples should be shown, especially when percentages are being used. Seventy-five per cent is an impressive statistical value, but if the full picture is that the sample was only 10 people, it is less so. Where quantities are indicated in the table, you must specify if they are in volumes or value. If numbers are used, specify the units. If currency is used, make sure that it is included in the table description.

Tables should be structured so that data is ordered from large to small items. The layout should enable data to be read easily. If data is imported, it should always be referenced or sourced. Tables should, if appropriate, contain

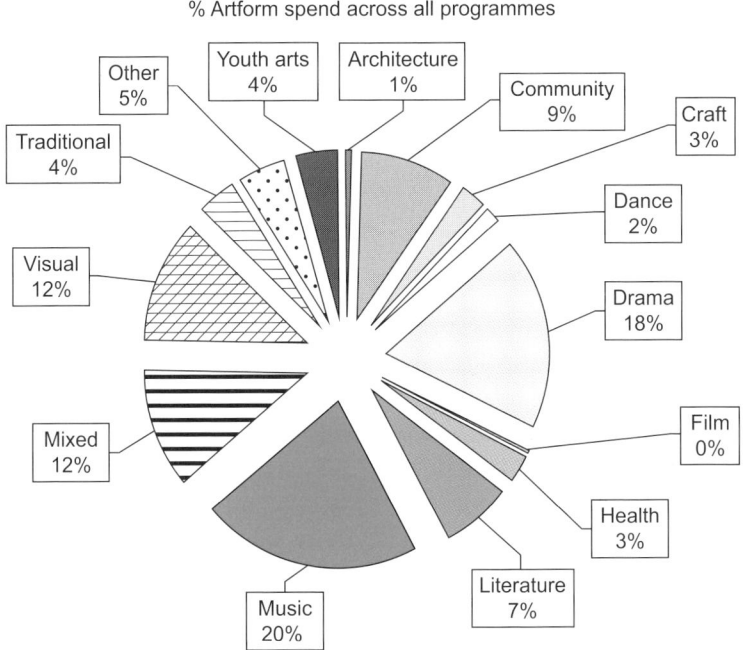

% Artform spend across all programmes

FIGURE 4.1

Example Pie Chart

totals and subtotals. Numbers should be right justified. You should normally work to two decimal places.

Other illustrative approaches should be examined and applied and can include pictograms, histograms, flow charts, graphs, bar charts and pie charts (Figure 4.1).

The development of diagrammatic illustration is further examined in Section 2.

ACTIVITY 4.1

Using the report template referred to above, take a reasonably small and short-term business activity or project and draft an outline-planning document using those headings listed.

SUMMARY

This chapter looked at the process of delivering results from research. It looked at the structure of a written research report and covered each of these. A certain emphasis was placed on diagrammatic illustration.

Senior Examiner's Comments – Section One

The Project Management in Marketing Unit dictates that students must have an appreciation and understanding of all the units at Level 4, as this knowledge will be relied upon, broadened and more deeply applied. With particular reference here, Unit 3 of the Professional Certificate in Marketing, Marketing Information and Research, is very important.

This section of the syllabus allows the student to contextualise research around a specific undertaking. Therefore, a relative understanding of the core fundamentals and principles is insufficient. Now, this must be developed and added to an ability to apply in context. The emphasis here is on the ability to disseminate varying amounts of information from disparate sources, identify gaps and consequently the rationale for primary research. As a result, the candidates should be able to manipulate their findings and present a justified case for the development and management of a specific marketing project.

In addition, the section explores the interface between the research brief and the research proposal and how this inter-relationship should manifest in an organisational mechanic that limits the risk of failure. The students must understand and appreciate how this applies in practice and will need to demonstrate their rigour in delivering and presenting these fundamental analyses.

Furthermore, the structure, format and illustration of findings are key to the final translation of any given marketing problem when managing solutions is the core business function. Therefore, a range of professional presentation tools needs to be explored, adapted and applied in context.

This section should equip the students with the necessary knowledge and skills to physically collect, manipulate and utilise marketing data and information. The students should prioritise undertakings and concentrate on their efforts. What needs to be researched and investigated will be highlighted through the assessment brief and nothing will be gained by straying from this. The students need to appreciate that no matter what the project, the data and information they collect from secondary sources will never be complete. This identifies the information gaps, which in turn, formulates the rationale for primary research.

It is important that the primary research undertaking is highlighted within student submissions for assessment.

From an assessment perspective, the emphasis within this subject area concentrates around the ability to recognise problems and identify research requirements. The matching of these through various methodologies will be the key and there will be an expectation that some form of primary undertaking is conducted and evidenced. The writing up and reporting of findings in a professional manner will be imperative, and the wide and varied use of illustrative diagrams and models within the presentation will be rewarded.

This section of the unit will directly impact the summary, critical analysis and prioritisation of findings.

- Concentration on primary data collection instruments, techniques and practical application is very important here.

Bibliography for Section 1

American Marketing Association (1961) *Report of the Definitions Committee*, (Quoted in Chisnall, P. (2004), *Marketing Research*, McGraw-Hill, 7th edition). AMA, Chicago.

Baker, S. and Mouncey, P. (2003) The market researcher's manifesto. *International Journal of Market Research*, 45(4), 415–33.

Chisnall, P. (2004) *Marketing Research*, 7th edition. McGraw-Hill, Maidenhead.

Crouch, S. and Housden, M. (2003) *Marketing Research for Managers*, 3rd edition. Elsevier Butterworth-Heinemann, Oxford.

Davenport, T. and Prusak, L. (1998) *Working Knowledge: How Organisations Manage What They Know*, (Quoted in Yahya and Goh (2002)). Harvard Business School Press.

Davidson, H. (1997) *Even More Offensive Marketing*. Penguin, Harmondsworth.

Dawson, C. (2003) Creative Business. *Financial Times*, 18 November.

De Tienne, K. and Thompson, J. (1996) Database marketing and organisational learning theory: towards and research agenda. *Journal of Consumer Marketing*, 13(5).

Jones, T. and Sasser, W. (1995) Why satisfied customers defect. *Harvard Business Review*, 73, 88–99.

Kotler, P. et al (2007) *Principles of Marketing*, 4th European edition. Prentice Hall Europe, Harlow.

Malhotra, Y. (1998) Deciphering the knowledge management hype. *Journal for Quality and Participation*, 21. (Quoted in Yahya and Goh (2002))

Reichheld, F.F. (2001) *The Loyalty Effect: The Hidden Force Behind Growth, Profits and Lasting Value*, revised edition. Harvard Business School Press, Watertown.

Wilson, A. (2006) *Marketing Research, An Integrated Approach*, 2nd Edition. FT Prentice Hall.

Wysocki, R.K., Beck, R. Jr and Crane, D.B. (2000) *Effective Project Management*. John Wiley and Sons, New York, Chichester.

Yahya, S. and Goh, W. (2002) Managing human resources for knowledge management. *Journal of Knowledge Management*, 6(5).

WEB SOURCES

Downer, G. (2002) *The Interactive and Direct Marketing Guide*, The IDM http://www.micromarketing-online.com. Experian (2003)

http://www.draytonbird.com/home

http://www.marketresearchworld.net/index.php?option=com_content&task=view
&id=2114&Itemid=78 last accessed 29.03.09

EXTENDING KNOWLEDGE

Books

Creswell, J.W. (2003) *Research Design: Qualitative, Quantitative and Mixed Method Approaches*, 2nd edition. Sage, Thousand Oaks.

Easterby-Smith, M., Thorpe, R. and Lowe, A. (2002) *Management Research: An Introduction*, 2nd edition. Sage, London.

Jankowicz, A.D. (1995) *Business Research Projects*, 2nd edition. Chapman & Hall, London.

McDaniel, C. and Gates, R. (2007) *Marketing Research Essentials*. John Wiley & Sons Inc, Minneapolis/St. Paul.

Articles

Catterall, M. and MacLaren, P. (2002) Researching consumers in virtual worlds: a cyberspace odyssey. *Journal of Consumer Behaviour*, 1(3), 228–38.

Kotler, P., Gregor, W. and Rogers, W. (1977) The marketing audit comes of age. *Sloan Management Review*, 18(2), 25–43.

Levitt, T. (1960) Marketing myopia. *Harvard Business Review*, July–August.

Building a Case for Marketing Projects (Weighting 20%)

LEARNING OBJECTIVES

By the end of this section, you will be able to:

- Prioritise and formalise business case objectives
- Prepare accurate and quantified forecasts and projections
- Understand customer profiling and scoring
- Appreciate resource requirements and tactical implementation
- Construct a case around core justifications

CHAPTER 5

Setting Aims, Goals and Objectives

"If we could first know where we are, then whither we are tending, we could then decide what to do and how to do it".
Abraham Lincoln, 1809–1865

INTRODUCTION

In Chapter 3, we considered the example of building a presentation and report as a response to a marketing research brief. That constituted a project with clear SMART objectives and the ability to measure outcomes against them. Project management, we must remember, is an organised process where the ideas apply to all projects, large or small.

With many large projects almost, the first step is to break them down into a series of smaller sub-projects. A large project may be complex to manage, and extended time frames can create a less focused feeling within the team as there appears to be a lot of time left; progress made seems insignificant compared to the size of the overall task, and it can be disheartening.

Consider briefly a full marketing plan. A strategic direction is chosen on the basis of information from a marketing audit. Detailed ideas are then considered to determine how to implement the strategy. These are evaluated and comparative risk/rewards ratios weighed up. From that process, a full implementation plan involving the marketing mix (and within that the promotional mix) is drawn up. Resources are committed and the plan is put into action. This is reviewed to monitor progress and ensure that it will meet the targets initially established.

However, within that broad overall picture, one team may have been given the task of researching information to found the marketing audit upon. That is the extent of their project. Another group may have been given the specific job of developing the segmentation, targeting and positioning (STP – see Chapter 7), while agencies may be invited to pitch for the business of preparing a promotional campaign to reposition the product or service as a result of the analysis. Their first project will be to prepare a successful pitch. If they do that, the next project is the actual campaign itself.

It is important to appreciate that the project management techniques are rarely a stop–start approach as so much within the modern business world is based on projects. A disciplined and logical approach is what is offered by the techniques, but this is only as a structure to achieve the individual marketing objectives discussed in the previous paragraph.

■ It is imperative when building cases and proposing projects that we consistently work with formalised and quantified objectives. There can be no ambiguity, and a focused and driven mechanic must dominate whenever we are justifying the necessity for investment and action. With this, all cases for functional activity become more feasible and viable.

WHERE ARE WE NOW?

We are still within the conceptual phase of the project life cycle – building the preliminary evaluation to guide the decision as to what is feasible.

In the process of establishing the facts and the situation surrounding any given marketing problem, a systematic and rigorous examination of the business environments impacted by the problem as well as the specific core elements relative to the problem will have been undertaken.

The whole aspect of information collection, analysis and management was considered in the previous section. With this in mind, there should be no doubt as to the importance of that research and the subsequent manipulation of the data that results whenever we are trying to build our business cases for marketing.

However, whenever we are dealing with this specific type of research geared towards a specific problem and requiring a specific project, it is unlikely that all the required data and information will be available from secondary sources alone.

THE POTENTIAL WEAKNESSES AND LIMITATIONS OF SECONDARY DATA

1. It is not related to the research question and the temptation may be to force the data to fit the question.

2. It may not be directly comparable. This is particularly the case in international markets where markets may be defined differently. For example, data on the low-alcohol drinks market varies from market to market as definitions of 'low' alcohol change.

3. Data may be incomplete. For example, the cross-channel trade in drinks and tobacco is significant but not included in official statistics.

4. Data may relate to certain markets – for example, data on food markets may relate to the retail trade rather than to the retail and catering markets, or vice versa. Pan-national studies will certainly find this. In many countries, a significant amount of the retail trade is made through street markets. This is very hard to quantify. In this case, it may be possible to weight data or use other techniques to complete the data set.

5. It may not be available. It may be that there are certain markets that are not adequately covered – for example, in Europe, data on the Belgian or Dutch market is often hard to obtain, as these are relatively small markets within the European Union.

6. The data may have been gathered for a particular purpose. Production statistics in certain markets are unreliable. Data may be presented to portray a company or government in a more favourable light. We see this in the United Kingdom, with the ongoing debate of how unemployment figures should be presented.

7. Information that is reviewed without access to the methodology should be viewed with suspicion and other data sources should be brought in to confirm the data under review.

8. Data for international markets may be more expensive and unreliable.

9. Data for international markets may be in a foreign language. Translating costs in business markets are very expensive.

10. Time series data may be interrupted by definition changes, for example, the most recent announcement by the British government about changes to the way inflation is calculated.

11. Secondary data in certain markets may not be up to date.

ACTIVITY 5.1

Reflect on the definitions of secondary research. What problems do you think the researcher may experience in using secondary data?

In fact, experience suggests that around 80% of the core information may be available around specifics, which therefore leaves a significant gap to be filled. In order to build cases, these gaps cannot exist. We must fill them if we are to succeed in fully justifying and quantifying our proposals in relation to organisational improvement or enhancement.

It is this mindset that enables us to define our discipline as an 'artistic science' or a 'scientific art'. This also adds weight to our proposals and allows us to flex our 'marketing muscles'.

Interrelated and interdependent on the previous section of the book, we will look here at the core primary undertakings we can engage in to fill our information gaps, be in a relatively full possession of the facts and build a quantifiably justified business case around our proposed business cases.

QUALITATIVE TECHNIQUES

Qualitative research accounts for between 10 and 15% of total research expenditure in the United Kingdom. It is growing in importance as marketing professionals recognise its vital role in providing depth of understanding about customers and their behaviour.

The Marketing Research Society (MRS) defines qualitative research as:

A body of research techniques which seeks insights through loosely structured, mainly verbal data rather than measurements. Analysis is interpretative, subjective, impressionistic and diagnostic.

Crouch and Housden's (2003) definition is: 'Qualitative research is so called because its emphasis lies in producing data which is rich in insight, understanding, explanation and depth of information, but which cannot be justified statistically'.

DATA-COLLECTION TECHNIQUES IN QUALITATIVE RESEARCH

Focus Groups or Group Discussions

Wilson (2006) defines group discussions as 'depth interviews with a group of people; they differ in that they involve interaction between respondents'.

MRS defines group discussions or focus groups as:

A number of respondents gathered together to generate ideas through the discussion of, and reaction to specific stimuli. Under the steerage of a moderator, focus groups are often used in exploratory work or when the subject matter involves social activities, habits and status.

Focus groups are generally made up of around 6–12 respondents. The most common number is 8. A lower number may be used when a particularly specialist topic is being discussed. The higher number would be used for a wide-ranging discussion. This design aspect is determined by the need to reflect the range of views held on a subject by the target market or concerned population.

They are run and managed by an interviewer, usually called a moderator. The moderator may be the same researcher who produced the research proposal, perhaps a specialist consultant or employed from a fieldwork agency. The moderator will control the group, keeping the discussion on track and probing for further information when needed. They will introduce other tasks that may occur within the group.

The main aim of the group is to ensure that the group members discuss the topic amongst themselves; the moderator's touch should be as light as possible. However, the skilled moderator will use a range of techniques to control the input of particularly vociferous members and to encourage quieter members of the group to make their contribution. Groups will normally last between 45 minutes and two hours. Discussions are generally tape-recorded or videoed.

Groups usually occur at the beginning of a research project as they can provide very useful information to explore through other methods. The groups may be observed remotely, and agencies offer clients the chance to view groups set up in special rooms, where the client can observe the group through a one-way window. A concealed or a discrete microphone to the observers can link the moderator so that a particularly interesting line of discussion can be probed further.

DEPTH INTERVIEWS

Depth interviews involve structured or semi-structured conversations or interviews with individuals directly involved with or having an impact upon the problem in question. The topic for discussion can be singular or multifaceted and closed or open-ended. The broad aims are relatively similar to those of the group discussions outlined above, but are primarily used when either it is not feasible to organise a group discussion or the presence of other people will not necessarily illicit deep and truthful responses from an individual or if the individual in question holds significant power and/or influence on or over the problem at hand.

In both approaches, the content for the topic of discussion relative to building a case will be formed by the detail within the gaps identified via the secondary desk research.

Of course, relative care must be taken when trying to manipulate the resultant data here, as the sample sizes are usually quite small and there can be a tendency and a temptation to over report the more sensational and disproportionate results and responses.

However, it is this addition to our data collection and manipulation that adds weight, support and justification to everyday marketing cases.

Therefore, to all intents and purposes, a robust statement of the situation pertaining to a specific case can be presented with confidence. Without this, cases cannot be built let alone proposed. If we have no idea about where we are, we have no opportunity to suggest where we should be. If we cannot state where we want to get to, then no case exists. That is why, to get to a stage whereby the case can sustain itself on its own merits, the rigour involved in this first stage of the build is imperative. More than likely, this will involve several data-collection rounds, several data gap analyses, several primary undertakings and multiple manipulations.

Nothing can guarantee success, but we can try to limit our risk of failure.

WHERE DO WE WANT TO BE?

Now that the foundations of the case are in place, we can proceed with the previously referred to confidence. With this diagnosis, project prescriptions can be written and the solutions to the problem as outcomes or deliverables can be quantified and formalised via the objectives. These objectives must be SMART and centred with no ambiguity while at the same time being capable of deep and severe cross-examination.

S   SPECIFIC
M MEASURABLE
A ACHIEVABLE
R REALISTIC
T TIMESCALED

Objectives must be able to fully stand up to SMART criteria. If they do not, they are not objectives and simply become only broad aims or goals. Broad aims or goals do not define business cases. Fully formalised and quantified SMART objectives do.

ACTIVITY 5.2

■ Download or refer to other published material that states or highlights the objectives for your own organisations or an organisation of your choice. Alternatively or in addition refer to the objectives you have set for yourself or for others.

■ Constructively criticise these using SMART criteria.

■ How many are robust enough to stand up to the test?

The majority of the marketing projects we have to build cases for are going to concentrate on the core areas of customers, management and profit. It stands to reason therefore that the cases we build for these projects must be focused and polished.

Customer objectives will be about market share, market development and market penetration. The emphasis will be on more customers, more business, retained business, new business and so on. Remember here, objectives could be about internal customers or even about divesting customers. Either way, and no matter the case or the project, customer objectives are entirely that, customer objectives, or any other physical manifestation of business transactions, that is consumers, clients, subscribers, end-users etc.

Management objectives will be about organisation and structure, systems and processes and culture and orientation. The emphasis will be on flatness and integration, technology and application and areas like customer focus, corporate social responsibility and ethics.

Profit objectives, depending upon how profit is defined, will concentrate on the bottom line, singular or triple, extracting cost out of the business, productivity, lifetime value, efficiency, economy of scale and shareholder value to name but a few.

It is important, when building and ultimately presenting business cases, that these objectives are clearly visible and overly explicit.

SUMMARY

In this chapter, we continued with the theme that a rigorous approach to the manipulation of marketing information is a management imperative if we are to be in a position to build business cases for our marketing projects. We established that secondary research creates information gaps relative to our marketing problems and that these can be filled somewhat by qualitative primary research. Having collected, analysed and manipulated the data to its fullest extent, we now appreciate we are in a position to formally state a position that will deliver a solution. This is formalised through our SMART objectives, which from a customer, management or profit perspective, must be up front and central.

CHAPTER 6

Forecasts and Projections

"I often say that when you can measure what you are speaking about, and express it in numbers, you know something about it; but when you cannot measure it, when you cannot express it in numbers, your knowledge is of a very meagre and unsatisfactory kind".

William Thomson, Lord Kelvin, 1824–1907

INTRODUCTION

Every manager, director, MD and owner in every business up and down the land, no matter what industry or sector, will utter these words 'OK! What's in this for us'? when faced with proposals to instigate any sort of investment in or change to the organisation. In fact, it is the statement that necessitates the diligence required in building business cases.

If we cannot present or articulate the answer to this question instantaneously, then no case exists.

In this chapter, we will examine some core tools and techniques that allow us to respond in a heartbeat. Depending upon the specific nature of the marketing project that is being considered, we may be either in the conceptual or the planning phase of the life cycle.

If we are using the following tools as part of the preliminary decision making, then we would be in the conceptual phase, but it could also be that the project is approved and this is more detailed research work to support decisions in actually making the plan.

FORECASTING IN MARKETING

One of the underlying fundamentals of marketing management is the opportunity to be able to try and predict and extrapolate future trends relative to areas such as demand, sales levels, seasonal variability, resource requirements, inventory and capacity to name but a few.

Without viable projections related to our marketing problems, we would be unable to build, let alone justify, any business case for onward adoption of our proposals. Therefore, we must investigate the alternative methods available to us to make these projections and utilise and apply those most compatible with our own specific problems.

JUDGEMENTAL FORECASTING

Judgemental forecasts are drawn from the subjective opinions of internal personnel like key employees, managers or directors, or external individuals like experts or academics. These opinions are collated, manipulated, aggregated and averaged in order to instigate some form of consensus that in turn will aid predicting trends and events in the future.

Two of the more widely used, delphi (also shown as capital lettered Delphi) method and sales force composite are outlined below.

DELPHI METHOD

The Delphi method is an attempt to 'align' the sometimes conflicting positions of experts into a coherent and unified perspective.

The Delphi method is based on a structured process for collecting and synthesising knowledge from a group of experts by means of a series of questionnaires accompanied by controlled opinion feedback. The questionnaires are presented in the form of an anonymous and consultation procedure by means of surveys (postal and/or email).

The technique is relatively simple. It consists of a series of questionnaires sent to a preselected group of experts. These questionnaires are designed to elicit and develop individual responses to the task specified and to enable the experts to refine their views as the groups work progresses in accordance with the assigned task. The rationale behind the Delphi method is to address and overcome the disadvantages of traditional forms of 'consultation by committee', particularly those related to group dynamics.

Delphi is primarily used to facilitate the formation of a group judgement. It was developed in response to problems associated with conventional group-opinion assessment techniques, such as Focus Groups, which can create problems of response bias owing to the dominance of powerful opinion leaders (Wissema, 1982). It may be used in forward planning to establish hypotheses about how scenarios are likely to develop, and on their socio-economic implications. For example, it has been widely used to generate forecasts in technology, education, and other fields. Fundamentally, the method serves to shed light on the evolution of a situation, to identify priorities or to draw up prospective scenarios.

The Main Steps Involved

The approach consists of questioning the experts by means of successive questionnaires, in order to reveal convergence and any consensus there may be.

The main stages of this process are:

Step 1 Determination and formulation of questions

Particular care should be given to the choice of questions, so as to obtain useful and applicable information.

Step 2 Selection of experts

These must have specific knowledge about the subject and be prepared to engage in this type of process.

Step 3 Formulation of a first questionnaire that is sent to the experts

The first questionnaire must contain a reminder of the nature of the study and include both semi-open and open questions.

Step 4 Analysis of the answers to the first questionnaire

The answers are analysed by someone other than the experts in order to determine the general trends and the most disproportionate answers.

Step 5 Formulation of a second questionnaire that is sent to experts

Each expert is informed of the results of the first round and is then asked to provide a new answer and to justify it if it differs from the general emerging themes and trends.

Step 6 Sending of a third questionnaire

This questionnaire can be a further manipulation based on Step 5. Sufficient convergence of opinions generally appears with this questionnaire. If that is not the case, the cycle continues.

Step 7 Summary of the process and drawing up of the final report.

It is important to note that the analysis of data elicited through Delphi surveys should be carried out using statistical analysis (e.g. cluster analysis or correlation analysis) in order to identify convergence and divergence in responses.

SALES FORCE COMPOSITE

In this method, sales personnel project volume of usage by customers in their area, territory or portfolio. The good thing about it is that the estimates are given by those people closest to the customer and also the method lends itself to product augmentation, territory development and penetration and customer segmentation, targeting and positioning.

The disadvantages are that sales persons are often not aware of broad economic forces, and also they may be evaluating sales performance and not necessarily forecasting per se, so they do not expend enough time and effort on the exercise. Also, there is a big aspect of potential bias, where there is a tendency to usually underestimate in order to make any resultant sales targets easier to achieve.

As the foremost customer-facing element of the business, sales professionals are extremely close to the market, demand, needs and requirements, emerging trends and potential macroenvironmental impacts.

TIME SERIES FORECASTING

Time series forecasting involves the deep and rigorous analysis of historical business data in order to establish and identify significant trends over time and fully explained via variance impact analysis. This technique and approach can then be utilised to extrapolate future results relative to specific scenarios or projects. The assumption is made that past patterns in the data can be used to forecast future data points (Figure 6.1).

FIGURE 6.1

Example Time Series Data

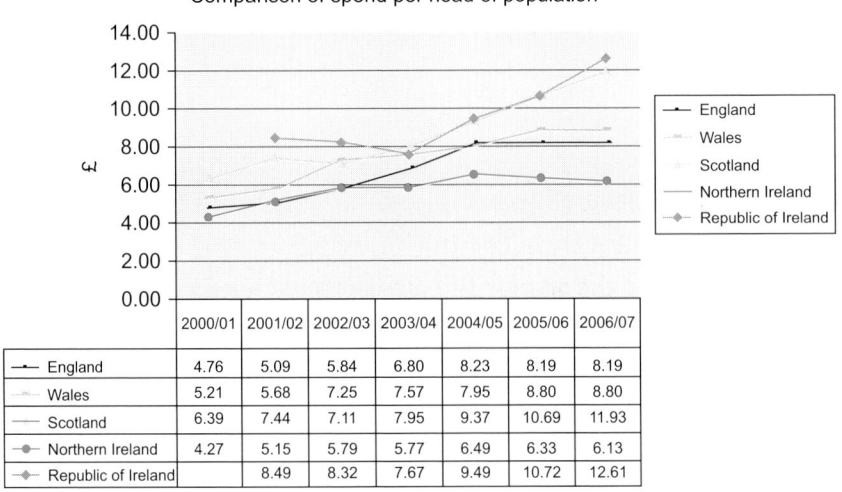

Comparison of spend per head of population

	2000/01	2001/02	2002/03	2003/04	2004/05	2005/06	2006/07
England	4.76	5.09	5.84	6.80	8.23	8.19	8.19
Wales	5.21	5.68	7.25	7.57	7.95	8.80	8.80
Scotland	6.39	7.44	7.11	7.95	9.37	10.69	11.93
Northern Ireland	4.27	5.15	5.79	5.77	6.49	6.33	6.13
Republic of Ireland		8.49	8.32	7.67	9.49	10.72	12.61

Some of the more widely used options are outlined below.

Moving Averages

1. The forecast is based on an arithmetic average of a given number of past data points and contains the following parameters and definitions:
2. An average is the mean of the observations over time.
3. A trend is a gradual increase or decrease in the average over time.
4. A seasonal influence is a predictable short-term cyclical pattern due to time of day, week, month, season, year etc.
5. A cyclical movement is a predictable long-term cyclical pattern due to a business cycle or product/service life cycle.
6. A random error is any remaining variation that cannot be explained by the other four components.

Simple Moving Average

Moving average techniques forecast demand by calculating an average of actual demands from a specified number of prior periods. Each new forecast drops the demand in the oldest period and replaces it with the demand in the most recent period; thus, the data in the calculation 'moves' over time.

Simple moving average: For example, consider a simple two-month average forecast model.

$$\text{Forecast of June sales} = \frac{\text{April sales} + \text{May sales}}{2}$$

$$= \frac{800 + 600}{2} = 700\ (1-2)$$

The more periods over which the moving average is calculated, the less susceptible the forecast is to random variations, but the less responsive it is to changes.

Weighted Moving Average

A weighted moving average is a moving average where each historical demand may be weighted differently.

Exponential Smoothing

Exponential smoothing gives greater weight to demand in more recent periods and less weight to demand in earlier periods, but in this method we do not have to save the values for many periods like the moving average methods. We just need the forecast and actual value for the current period and then we would be able to forecast the value for the next period.

SEASONAL METHODS

What happens when the patterns you are trying to predict display seasonal effects?

What is seasonality? It can range from true variation between seasons to variation between months, weeks, days in the week and even variation during a single day or hour. To deal with seasonal effects in forecasting, two tasks must be completed:

A forecast for the entire period must be made using whatever forecasting technique is appropriate. This forecast will be developed using whatever the forecast must be adjusted to reflect the seasonal effects in each period.

The seasonal method adjusts a given forecast by multiplying the forecast by a seasonal factor.

These approaches by nature lend themselves more to the short-term aspect of forecasting.

ACTIVITY 6.1

- Using any historical data at your disposal, try and apply some time series analysis to it.

CAUSAL FORECASTING

Causal forecasting examines changes caused by fluctuations in one or more variables. Such variables may extend to but not be exclusive to such elements as competitor activities, price variations, supply shortages and so on. So with this extended analysis, time is not the only variable investigated.

Some of the more common techniques for this type of forecasting are outlined below.

CORRELATION AND REGRESSION

The purpose of correlation analysis is to determine whether there is a relationship between two sets of variables. We may find that:

- There is a positive correlation.
- There is a negative correlation.
- There is no correlation.

Example   **49**

Correlation and regression are concerned with the investigation of two variables.

Correlation describes the strength of the relationship. It is not concerned with 'cause' and 'effect'.

Regression describes the relationship itself in the form of a straight-line equation that best fits the data.

Previously, we have only considered a single variable; now, we look at two associated variables.

We might want to know:

- Does a relationship exist between these variables?
- How strong that relationship is.
- What constitutes the relationship?
- Will the strength of the relationship be sufficient to aid predictions or forecasts?

EXAMPLE

The figures represent the sales for a particular firm of manufacturers and also the average monthly temperature.

Month	Av. temp. (°C)	Sales (£000,000)
January	3	74
February	5	58
March	6	82
April	7	95
May	13	111
June	14	125
July	17	135
August	16	140
September	13	125
October	10	104
November	6	82
December	4	81

Some initial insight into the relationship between two continuous variables can be obtained by plotting a scatter diagram and looking at the resulting graph.

Does the relationship seem to be linear or curved?

Scatter diagram

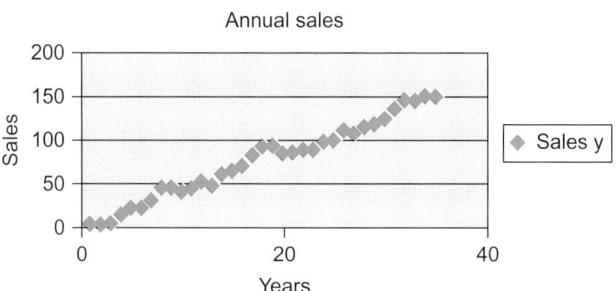

If there appears to be a linear relationship, it can be quantified and a correlation therefore exists.

If the relationship is found to be significantly strong, then its nature can be found using linear regression, which defines the equation of the straight line of best fit through the data.

For example, £x spent on Advertising would be expected to increase Sales by y%.

The best fit can be calculated to see how well the line fits the data.

Once defined by this equation, the relationship can be used for forecasting purposes (Figure 6.2).

In practice, there seems to be a tendency to favour the potential accuracy of causal approaches as opposed to judgemental approaches. In relation to judgemental techniques, no one technique is more favourable or reliable, but the Delphi method is most popular. Time series analysis is more robust when more variables are examined simultaneously. Correlation and regression analysis is well used and accepted. However, no singular method is superior and the practised forecaster will use a combination of tools at their disposal.

SUMMARY

We have established here that without significant projections as to future outcomes based on acceptable forecasting techniques, potentially our business cases could not stand up to intense scrutiny. Whether judgemental, time series or causal, our approach to forecasting should be relevant, applicable and varied.

CHAPTER 7

Operational Management

INTRODUCTION

The central core running through the business cases we construct to support our marketing projects will contain common themes and content.

Consequently, we must consider, analyse and assess major relevance to the case around customer or other stakeholder groupings, the marketing tools and techniques utilised in pursuit of better businesses and the resource capabilities and capacity required as input.

SEGMENTATION, TARGETING AND POSITIONING

As a general rule, no business case will be in a position to ignore the whole underlying aspect of power and influence that permeates throughout marketing projects. Whether that is a customer, internal or external, other stakeholders, internal or external, the fundamental principles of segmentation, targeting and position will be the foundations and cornerstones that a case can be built around.

The basic premise here is that we cannot be all things to all men. As a result, we need to drill down and concentrate our efforts and resources on where the best opportunity for success exists.

SEGMENTATION

What needs to be established from the outset is the population in its entirety. This is the big picture whereby we can deconstruct it to its lowest common denominators. We must try and establish clusters of homogeneous entities in order to proceed with a process of exploiting opportunities.

The case therefore begins by reducing a potential disaggregation.

CASE EXAMPLE – Harley Davidson

Harley Davidson is revving up efforts to broaden its appeal to younger riders and women. Though its initiatives are ongoing, the company has paved the way with some success. Women have grown from about 5% of the brand's retail buyers in the mid-1990s to about 10% today, and sales to Gen Xers are growing eight times faster than to Harley's traditional demo. Harley is now pursuing younger male buyers and female customers in several ways. It reaches out to the dreamers group through a direct mail program. Advertising is also playing a major role in refining the Harley brand. Harley marketers are using humour in ads to convey the brand's aspirational message, as well as to court new target demos. For many owners, the Harley experience is about the enjoyment and camaraderie of being on the open road. So, the Harley Owners Group has become an integral part of Harley's PR and Marketing.

But the Milwaukee-based company, which turned 100 last year, is not standing still. Rather, it is revving up efforts – launching new products and ad strategies, as well as grass roots programs – to broaden its appeal to younger riders and women.

'We have very high brand awareness and appeal among all demographic groups, but being a big-ticket item for a discretionary purpose, some people say there's no rational reason to buy a Harley', said Tom Watson, Harley's director of marketing. 'We're trying to make our brand and products relevant in new and meaningful ways to a group we've loosely identified as "dreamers", who say they want to ride some day and own a Harley Davidson'.

According to the company, the median age of new Harley buyers increased to about 46 last year, from just under 45 in 1999. At the same time, the median income rose to about $80,000 last year, compared to $72,500 in 2007.

Harley is now pursuing younger male buyers and female customers in several ways. It reaches out to the 'dreamers' group, for example, through a direct mail program. When a potential customer contacts Harley through a business-reply card or online, the company mails back an 'Attainability Program' packet that includes information about products, financing arrangements and local dealerships. 'We want to get these people across the threshold', Watson noted. 'They may not buy this year or next year, but this keeps them aware'.

Article: Can Harley Ride the New Wave? *Dale Buss*. Brandweek. New York: Oct 25, 2004. Vol. 45, Iss. 38; pg. 20, 3 pgs. (Figure 7.1).

FIGURE 7.1

Sample population classification

Market segments
A – Wholesaler/retailer
B – Business services
C – Trade professional

In order to do this, several bases for segmentation must be established. If we think about the traditional use of segmentation, these are bases such as demographic, geographic and socio-economic on the quantitative side and psychographic on the qualitative side. What defines these bases, however, are the nature and scope of the project, the objectives and the deliverables.

The more bases for segmentation that is used therefore, the stronger the overall case will be evidenced.

Once the segmentation bases have been selected, we must apply them and segment the population under question (Tables 7.1–7.2).

Whenever we have our population segmented, we need to score the clusters or segments for attractiveness. Here, we set a hierarchy of attractiveness criteria, which in turn becomes our central case for targeting.

Table 7.1   Expanded population

Segments	Business classification
A – Wholesaler/retailer	Jewellers, fashion outlets, health foods, crafts, motoring, home furnishing, DIY, chemicals, agricultural, poultry, sporting, computer store
B – Business services	Hotels, travel agents, estate agents, care, finance, construction, digital services, car hire, tour operators, motoring, insurance
C – Trade professionals	Joiners, plumbers, electricians, gardeners, catering, party supplies, hair salons, oil & gas, equipment hire

Table 7.2   Segmentation bases

Bases	Definitions
Business size	Small to medium businesses (1–10 employees)
Geographic location	Local, regional
Business type	Internet based, retail shop, office based, home office
Methods of promotion	Internet, newspaper, magazine, directories

ACTIVITY 7.1

For a stakeholder population of your choice, use the table below to think about numerous characteristics relative to different qualitative variables.

Variables	Characteristics
Choice criteria	
Benefit sought	
Decision-making structure	
Decision-making process	
Buy class	
Purchase pattern	
Attitude towards Internet marketing	
Market growth	
Information needs	
Attitude to change	
Teamworking	
Cultural orientation	
Innovation	

TARGETING

The scoring criterion again is defined by the project to which the process refers, and will vary from project to project. Having defined the criteria fully, we can proceed to score (Table 7.3).

As a result of our scoring mechanisms, identifiable targets present themselves via a fully quantifiable and justified process. The robustness of our case becomes manifest (Table 7.4).

Now we are presenting a case grounded in fundamental techniques, having introduced a scientific approach to our justifications. The final aspect of the case in this instance is to always remember our approach to positioning.

POSITIONING

All that needs to be established here is the mindset of the population and any competing entities or variables. Figure 7.2 gives a typical B2C commercial positioning statement.

We must always remember that a process of segmentation, targeting and positioning for building and justifying cases should always go hand in hand and cannot be a stand-alone approach. That is, it is not just about segmentation – it is about segmentation, targeting and positioning.

Table 7.3 Attractiveness criterion

Criteria scoring	Most attractive	Attractive	Average	Below average
Profit	10	8	5	3
Competition				
Ability to serve				
Proximity				
Economics of scale				
Change programme				
Barriers				
Resources				

Table 7.4 Target identification

Segmentation	Wholesaler/retailer	Business services	Trade professionals
	A	B	C
Score	99	49	21

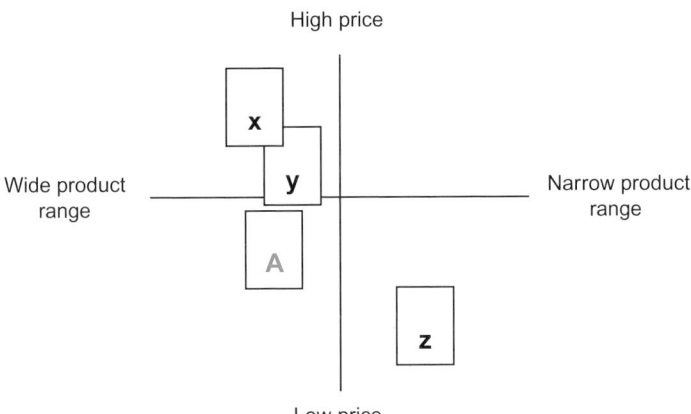

FIGURE 7.2
Positioning map

This sequential and consequential approach to building a business case in support of our proposed marketing projects also needs to recognise that different scenarios and situations will demand changes to how we manage our marketing tools and techniques in the face of specific undertakings. Integration is of course the key, and we need to recognise and identify the indicators within our case-building activities.

THE PRODUCT

Always remember to define this in relation to the offer that is made available for consumption. Business case justifications will concentrate on new product development or the reigniting of the product life cycle.

THE PRICE

Always remember to define this as the consideration necessary to transact the consumption. Justifications will concentrate on skimming and penetration.

THE PLACE

Defined as a location or a distribution process or making available what is on offer for consumption. The justification here is normally about extracting transaction out the channels.

THE PROMOTION

Defined as communicating what is on offer for consumption. Our business cases here concentrate on push, pull and profile aspects of our integrated marketing communications mix.

In addition, the elements of People, Processes and Physical evidence will also need to be moulded to determine the extent to which the mix needs to be amended or adjusted for any particular project case. We will look at the People aspect here in more depth.

MANAGING DYNAMICS

There are often many changes over the period of the project. These changes are referred to as 'dynamics'. Irrespective of the methodology, managing project dynamics is key to a project's successful completion. Changes can result from:

External market dynamics – such as changes in competitors, the size and value of the market, the potential media or routes to market.

The business dynamics – such as business priorities, resource levels, personnel, interactions with stakeholders, including suppliers and customers.

Project dynamics – such as the interaction of factors influencing costs and schedules on the specific project, and the interaction of the people within the project.

Managing dynamics is central to the agile project approaches. However, even process methodologies will have to manage some aspects of project dynamics.

MANAGING PEOPLE

Project process and methodology rely on people to work towards the conclusion. While agile approaches take more account of the individual's views, both are dependent on people working together.

Here, we will look at some key elements of people issues in project management. First, we look at the role and skills of the project manager, then we look at managing the team.

PROJECT MANAGER

The most central role in the project is that of the project manager. Some organisations have identified the specific requirements for this role through skills/competency analysis. Table 7.5 summarises those identified in research across sectors linked with the problems that can arise when these skills and competencies are not in place.

Table 7.5 Project management skills and project management problems

Project management skills	Project management problems
Communication skills Listening Persuading	Breakdowns in communication
Organisational skills Planning Goal setting Analysing	Insufficient planning Inadequate resources
Team-building skills Empathy Motivation Esprit de corps	Team members uncommitted Weak interunit integration
Leadership skills Setting an example Energetic Vision (the big picture) Delegates Positive	Unclear goals/direction Interpersonal conflicts
Coping skills Flexibility Creativity Patience Persistence	Handling changes
Technological skills Experience Project knowledge	Meeting ('unrealistic') deadlines

Note: These generic categories of project management skills are identified in order of importance on the basis of a survey of project managers.
Source: From Pozner, B.Z. (1987) 'What it takes to be a good project manager', Project Management Journal.

ACTIVITY 7.2

The desired competencies and personal attributes of marketing personnel and project managers often differ.

Compare your skills and competencies with those for a project manager.

On the basis of this, what problems might you face when managing projects? How might you overcome these?

Does your organisation have specific project managers in marketing?

If so, identify the skills and competencies in the job requirements for these roles, and compare them with those for marketing roles.

THE PROJECT TEAM

Once the project manager is in place, the next manpower challenge is of forming the project team. Ideally, the project manager and the team should gel. However, problems may exist in this:

The different backgrounds and experiences of team members.

The availability of team members, especially where these are on temporary secondments or working part-time on the project.

The levels of commitment to the project, which may not be central to their main work.

Often, projects are formed on the basis of who is available for the projects. Ideally, these people should also be willing to work on this, but often this is not the case. This is an issue that can cause major problems, and indeed may be a key area for risk management review in the project.

Team roles may be defined within projects. These can be across the different functional disciplines or created from people with similar backgrounds to create synergy. There may be levels of teams for larger projects, with a core team, which is led by the project manager, and comprises the heads of key activity areas, or subteams, which are led by the heads of key activity areas, and which report to the project manager.

Ideally, team profiling, using for example Belbin, should be applied to the team. This is most appropriate for larger team projects, but it often identifies problems when appointing team members from within a marketing department (who may all have been appointed for similar roles within the marketing team).

Many consultants recommend an initial team-building activity when a project is first launched. However, this is not exclusive to the project launch – team-building events can help sustain a strong, motivated team. Remember that this can include team members from external agencies.

MANAGING TEAM PROBLEMS

Kezsbom (2001) reports that there are seven sources of conflict in managing teams. These are:

Project priorities – team members view the importance and flow of activities and tasks differently.

Administrative procedures – team members often have conflicting views over how the project should be managed or run.

Technical problems – team members disagree over technical matters, such as specifications, performance and priorities.

Resources – such as getting staff and computers from functional departments, and having access to shared services.

Cost – project manager and team members disagree over the costs of the WBS activities and tasks.

Schedules – project manager and team members disagree over the order and timing of project tasks.

Personality – managing interpersonal behaviour to create a culture of collaboration and respect.

ACTIVITY 7.3

Take each of Kezsbom's seven sources of conflict and consider these in relation to your organisation. Taking into account what you have studied on managing teams in the Managing Marketing module, think about how you would deal with problems that emerge in these areas.

Ultimately, it is the people who undertake the management and implementation of project work. A good project manager should have the skills and competencies to manage the team and the resulting problems, as this is the way that a project will be on target to meet the time and cost elements, and deliver to the required standards.

INVESTMENT AND INCOME

It stands to reason that no business case can be complete without fully quantified budgets. These are the 2I (Investment and Income) budgets that will highlight all the necessary financial resource required to be invested and have this detailed on a line-by-line basis and secondly show the expected and projected return on such investments over time.

If we assume the mantra of investing resources as opposed to being defined as a cost centre, we will never lose sight of the fact that it is a business case we are constructing and presenting.

These issues are examined in much more depth in your Managing Marketing course book and will aid your knowledge when developing robust cases.

The major investment measurement and proposal tools that you should be familiar with include:

Accounting rate of return (ARR)
Payback
Discounted cash flow
Net present value (NPV)
Internal rate of return
Return on investment (ROI)

SUMMARY

In this chapter, we were able to establish that the central core of our business cases will deal in a robust manner with a situation-specific population.

The management and metamorphosis of our marketing mix will be ever changing.

Core human and financial resources need to be managed within the confines of organisational capacity.

CHAPTER 8

The Case Report

INTRODUCTION

The case now needs to be presented and illustrated in a manner that enhances the case to its fullest extent, and invariably this will be both in written and verbal forms.

The structure and format for reporting outlined in Section 1 remains as the template here, but now needs to assume the personality of the constructor.

So, our concentration here will be on the use of illustrations and models and hints and tips for verbal presentations. The report or presentation (or both) can be required during any part of the project's life cycle. As with project management itself, they are merely mechanisms and techniques that support the work of the marketing effort – whatever that is at each stage.

DON'T WRITE IT UP, DRAW IT UP

Through whatever visual medium the report appears, Word or PowerPoint, the more hard-hitting illustrations we can introduce, the better.

So without further ado, let us practice what we preach. Shown following are a series of simple diagrams that illustrate the range and type of diagram that is available to the marketing practitioner (Figures 8.1–8.4).

Illustrations bring our reports and presentations to life and every picture paints a thousand words.

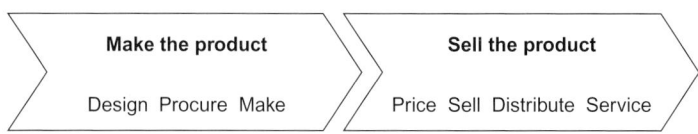

Physical process sequence

Value delivery system and relationships

Forward and backward movement of funds, information, materials and products

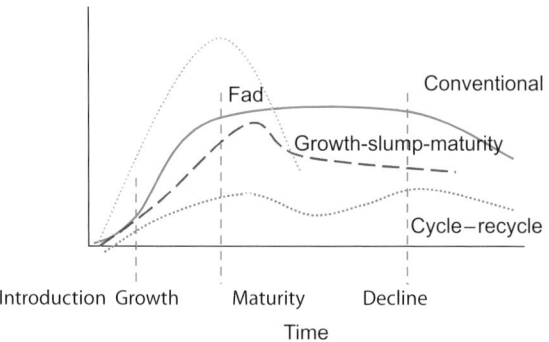

Different patterns of cycles

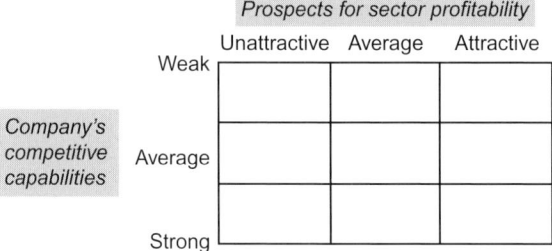

Multifactor matrix shell directional policy matrix

Presentation Tips

Wilson (2006) offers some handy tips, hints and techniques outlined below.

Meet your objectives. State them early on and show throughout how your presentation contributes to their achievement. You might even ask the audience what their objectives are at the beginning of the presentation, note them on a flip chart and at the end of the presentation tick them off.

Know your audience; what do they want to hear? How many will be present? Who are they? What positions do they hold?

How will you dress? Is it formal or informal or will you be overdressed in a suit and a tie? What do your audience expect?

Keep it brief and to the point, use a balanced mixture of words and images and keep to time.

Be prepared for interruptions and stop presenting if your audience are distracted. Do not plough on.

If using PowerPoint technology, make sure that it is compatible with the projection system. Make sure that your slides do not contain too much information and that tables and graphics can be read.

A further series of examples of the more popular type of graphics that can be used (amongst many others) is shown following.

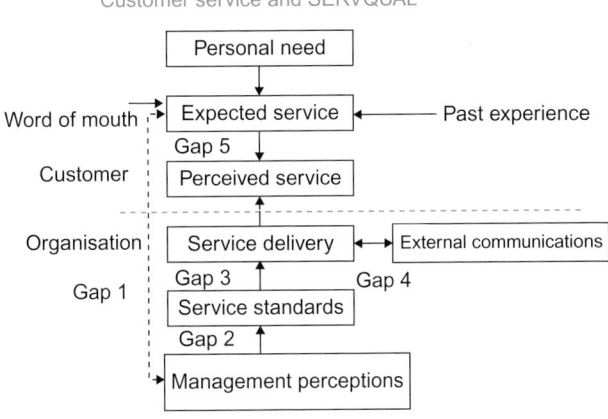

Customer service and SERVQUAL

FIGURE 8.5
The SERVQUAL model
Source: Zeithaml,
Parasuraman, Berry (88)

With the acknowledgement of the growth in importance of service, a method of measuring gaps in the performance of such services was developed.

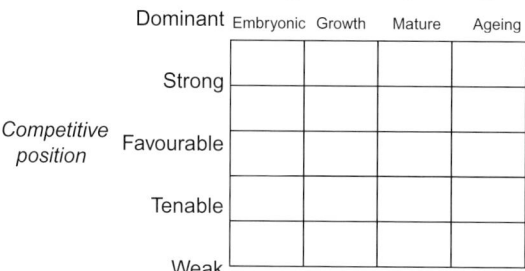

Arthur D. Little Strategic condition matrix

This diagram uses the elements of competitive position and industry maturity to help determine the current competitive position. From this, decisions as to future strategic direction can be based. The stages of industry maturity are often considered to have a parallel with the product life cycle (Figure 8.7).

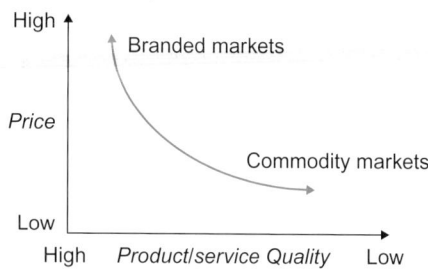

This type of diagram gives a simple, visual picture of how important the brand is within the overall value creation by plotting specified products or services onto the chart. Rapid comparison of those products can be carried out (Figure 8.8).

Task	Responsibility	Jan	Feb	Mar	Apr	May	Jun	Jul	Aug	Sep	Oct	Nov	Dec
Get funding													
Suppliers selection													
Plant													
Recruitment													
Skimming													
Product													
Marcomms													
Distribution													
Mkis													
Decor													
Feedback													

The diagram shows a very simple approach where stages are struck through as they are completed. More typically, they may be in the form of a Gantt chart, where the predicted schedule is shown as a bar on the calendar section, showing when and how long it is expected to take. Against that, a further bar shows the actual progress that has been made. Modern software allows for a great deal of 'drilling down' for more detail, but the higher level chart is still useful for giving a snapshot of what has happened and what remains to be done.

Expense	Description	Year 1	Year 2	Year 3	Year 4	Year 5
Sales*	Product and services	£256,000	£313,600	£337,000	£346,000	£349,600
Operating cost	Rental, wages, rates etc	£63,600	£68,052	£72,815	£77,912	£83,365
Marketing cost	Promo/trade shows/ads	£9,000	£11,000	£9,000	£11,000	£9,000
Total over/heads		£72,600	£79,052	£81,815	£88,912	£92,365
Net profit		£183,400	£234,548	£255,185	£257,088	£257,235

FIGURE 8.9

Investment/income budget

A simple pulling together of key accounting values in a table can help understanding, but further detailed investigation can be triggered from it.

MAINTAINING CONTROL OF THE PRESENTATION

During the presentation, maintain eye contact with your audience. Try to avoid having a physical barrier between you and your audience.

Be aware of your body language, relax your shoulders, smile and try to project enthusiasm.

Relax and use natural movements. Engage with your audience but do not invade their personal space.

Make eye contact with all the people in the room early in the presentation – get them on your side.

Face your audience rather than the screen. If you are able to, determine where each member of the team presenting and the audience will sit.

Never turn your back to the audience.

Do not hide behind lecterns and A4 notes.

Use cue cards if necessary, do not try to ad-lib unless you are well rehearsed. Be aware of your strengths and limitations and do not let your ego conflict with professionalism.

Provide handouts for your audience of the slides, tables and graphs that may be hard to read.

If working with a team of presenters, make sure that you support them. When you are not presenting, maintain a positive attitude and listen to the rest of the team. If a team member falters or technology is causing problems, act to sort out the situation. Do not sit there thinking, 'thank goodness that is not me'. You will be judged by the performance of the team as a whole.

Keep to time and take responsibility for your own timings. Some audiences for competitive pitches will stop a presentation if it overruns.

Use pictures, video and audio clips to enliven and add variety to the presentation, but do not make a presentation overbusy.

Research has shown that people forget 30% of what they are told after just three hours and 90% is forgotten after only three days. Visual aids can help and variety is the key. The combination of verbal and visual material has been shown to deliver 85% recollection after three hours and up to 65% after three days.

Almost all presentations are made using PowerPoint, and the lack of pacing and variety often creates a very flat atmosphere and passive audience. This is often the case as projection equipment may mean that the lights have to be dimmed and the audience sink into a soporific state. Popcorn might be a more appropriate snack than the executive biscuit selection. Liven it up by using a variety of support and dynamic pacing through the presentation – rather than trying to compensate by overly using graphics (slide transitions, animations etc.).

Practise, practise, practise, and remember 'fail to prepare, prepare to fail'.

Make sure you carry out a 'dress' rehearsal. Practise speaking out loud.

Practise all aspects of the presentation including the transition between speakers and the use of supporting technology or audio-visual aids.

It may help to record your rehearsal and pick up your verbal tics, the 'you knows', the 'hums' and the 'yes's'. Knowing that you have these verbal tics can help control them. Practise volume and pace and the use of silence.

Tell them what you will tell them, tell them and tell them what you have told them.

Structure the presentation by using staging posts and summarising slides to close sections and introduce new sections.

Always start and finish on a high note.

SUMMARY

If our cases are written in a report or presented in person, we must remember that we are pitching for the initiation of our projects. Care, dedication and rigour must be employed and aligned with confidence, ambition and passion.

Senior Examiner's Comments – Section Two

This section of the syllabus develops the case further by assessing the organisational potential and the impacts and implications on capabilities and resources. Whereas, at Level 3, the emphasis is on introducing the notion of control and then at Level 4, developing the imperative further, here we go much deeper. Building cases from a project management perspective is the ultimate control mechanism.

Candidates need to understand now that practising marketers are judged by their decision making and recommendations and are accountable for the associated outcomes. This is all about rigour and the courage of conviction. Marketing students and practitioners can be ultimately more courageous when in possession of a justified case.

Students must recognise and define via SMART criteria the deliverables to be achieved while at the same time recognising that control mechanisms are introduced from the outset and not as a 'bolt-on'. It is therefore necessary to express the vision in core terms of customers, management and profit. A point of note here is that 'profit' can be defined from a number of perspectives and does not exclusively relate to financial standards. What determines the definition is the nature and scope of the project.

Within the section, a framework exists for building the case and a sequenced approach maintains the mantra of 'limiting the risk of failure'. In other words, the evidence has been collected and synthesised. Now, it must be prepared and cross-examined. If a case exists, it can be presented. If it does not, more evidence is required.

Candidates are expected to evaluate relevant customer segments and clusters, critically rank and identify where the greatest impact exists and ensure that any given project fits within the mindset of the customer relative to the competition.

There needs to be recognition of the availability of scant resources, and the aspect here is to examine the structure, competence and capability of the organisation to implement and deliver. Having determined this, the student can recommend an operational fit that becomes the vehicle by which the objectives are met. This will necessitate the adaptation of the extended marketing mix to be compatible with the proposed project.

With this in place, operational budgets can be formulated that outline the resources required and projected returns. It is important here to be as accurate and detailed as possible. The detail of this analysis will justify the case.

At this level, there is no option for sitting on the fence and the examining team will be looking for a structured approach to building business cases.

As in Section 1, the presentation of the case is key and the formalised report should reflect this in a highly professional document.

From an assessment perspective, there are two aspects that are important.

First, where customers, management and profit are concerned, it is essential that formal SMART objectives are developed and associated projections and budgets presented. Without these value creating statements (both operational and financial), it is unlikely that any case would be justified or acceptable.

Second, but not exclusively, core recommendations should be grounded in the fundamental principles of segmentation, targeting and positioning. Value-creating solutions must be interdependent and compatible with context and resources. A cohesive and coherent operational fit within these core areas will be rewarded.

- A core understanding of and the ability to apply traditional forecasting, extrapolation and budgeting tools for both investment and income/profit in any given context is imperative here.

Bibliography for Section 2

Bower, M. and Garda, R.A. (1985) The role of marketing in management. *The Mckinsey Quarterly*, autumn, 34–46.

Collier, P.M. (2006) *Accounting for Managers*, 2nd edition. Wiley, Chichester.

Crouch, S. and Housden, M. (2003) *Marketing Research for Managers*. Elsevier, Oxford.

Doyle, P. (2000) *Value Based Marketing: Strategies for Corporate Growth and Shareholder Value*. Wiley, Chichester.

Drucker, P.F. (1993) *Management Tasks, Responsibilities, Practices*. Harper & Row, New York.

Gray, C.F. and Larson, E.W. (2008) *Project Management: The Managerial Process*, 4th edition. McGraw-Hill, London.

Jobber, D. (2007) *Principles and Practice of Marketing*, 5th edition. McGraw-Hill, London.

Kezsbom, D.S. (2001) People Issues. *AACE International, transactions 2001*, 1–2.

Lewis, J.P. (2007) *Mastering Project Management*, 2nd edition. McGraw-Hill, London.

Peter, J.P. and Olson, J.C. (2007) *Consumer Behaviour and Marketing Strategy*, 8th edition. McGraw-Hill, London.

Porter, M.E. (1980) *Competitive Strategy: Techniques for Analysing Industries and Competitors*. Free Press, New York.

Ward, K. (1989) *Financial Aspects of Marketing*. Heinemann, Oxford.

Wilson, A. (2006) *Marketing Research, An Integrated Approach*, 2nd edition. Prentice Hall, Harlow.

Wissema, J.G. (1982) Trends in technology forecasting. *R&D Management*, 12(1), 27–36.

Zeithaml, V. et al (1988) SERVQUAL: A multiple-item Scale for measuring customer perceptions of service quality, *Journal of Retailing*, 64(1), 12–40.

EXTENDING KNOWLEDGE

Articles

Firat, A.F. and Schultz, C.L. (1997) From segmentation to fragmentation. Marketing strategy in the postmodern era. *European Journal of Marketing*, 31(3/4), 183–207.

Hooley, G.J. et al (1992) Our five year mission: to boldly go where no man has been before. *Journal of Marketing Management*, 8(1), 35–48.

Kaplan, R.S. and Norton, D.P. (1992) The balanced scorecard: measures that drive performance. *Harvard Business Review*, 70(1), 71–79.

Kaplan, R.S. and Norton, D.P. (1993) Putting the balanced scorecard to work. *Harvard Business Review*, 71(5), 134–147.

Kaplan, R.S. and Norton, D.P. (2000) Having trouble with your strategy? Then map it. *Harvard Business Review*(September–October), 167–176.

Sanghera, S. (2005) Why so many mission statements are mission impossible. *Financial Times*(22nd July), 13.

Zadek, S. (1998) Balancing performance, ethics and accountability. *Journal of Business Ethics*, 17(October), 1421–1441.

Assessing, Managing and Mitigating Risk Associated with Marketing Projects (Weighting 25%)

3.1 Critically evaluate the importance of developing an understanding of risk assessments in organisations in order to protect long-term stability of a range of marketing projects

3.2 Critically evaluate the differences between the following types of organisational risk

3.3 Analyse and assess the potential sources of risk, of both internal and external origins, directly related to a specific case and consider the impact of these risks on the organisation

3.4 Design a risk management programme appropriate to measuring the impact of risk in the context of marketing projects

3.5 Undertake risk assessments on marketing projects and assess the impact of short-/long-term tactical changes to the marketing plan

3.6 Critically evaluate the different approaches an organisation can take to mitigate risk in order to reduce its potential to harm the organisation or its reputation

3.7 Critically assess the strategic impact of implementing proposed risk control measures vs. the strategic impact of taking no action

3.8 Develop a range of methods for monitoring, reporting and controlling risk on an ongoing basis for project implementation

Identifying Risk

Whatever can go wrong will go wrong
Murphy's Law

Murphy was an optimist
Thomas B and Housden M, 2002,
IDM course material, used with permission

*There are known knowns, known unknowns,
and unknown unknowns*
Donald Rumsfeld, 2003

*46% of FTSE 250 companies said it would take
less than a day for a serious disruption to impact
significantly on their business*

*While 46% of businesses are required by customers to show
they have business continuity measures in place, three
quarters now ask their own suppliers to do the same*
BSI Business Barometer, 2006 cited in BSI, 2009

INTRODUCTION

Risk is an inevitable part of life. To remove risk from our life and to live life fully is impossible. For most of us, the assessment and management of risk occurs almost subconsciously and draws on our experience and the application of common sense.

The year 2009 is the 200th anniversary of the birth of the great scientist Charles Darwin, whose theories transformed the way we think about our place on earth. Today, the Darwin Awards present in a tragic–comic way the unfortunate results of individuals failing to assess fully the risks attached to the decisions they make.

CASE EXAMPLE – Hoover

Hoover Sucks

'The Hoover promotion has been described as "Britain's worst marketing disaster" and one that promoters should have learned from. The results of this promotion could have and should have been easily avoided if the risk management industry's advice had been adhered to and the promoter had incorporated necessary risk management steps when the promotion was first put together'.

Source: Brand republic, 2009, weblink: www.brandrepublic.com/News/210917/lot-learn-Hoover-free-flights-fiasco/

In marketing and business, the ability to assess, manage and mitigate risk has never been more important. Over the next few years, as we leave a period of high growth in many sectors, during which many of us have seen marketing budgets increase alongside sales, and enter a recession widely feared to be the worst for several generations, the need to manage the risks that might threaten the successful delivery of marketing projects becomes more important. There are many examples of the failure to manage risks effectively.

Remember that the ability to assess risk and to react effectively is fundamental, not just within project management, but as a basic prerequisite for business survival.

Let us look at a few examples of what can go right and what can go wrong.

The quotation above refers to a promotional campaign where the purchase of a new Hoover vacuum cleaner gave 'free flights'. The value of such flights was often greater than the cost of the cleaner, and many bought them simply to reduce their travel costs. The company was taken to court when they tried to find legal loopholes that reduced their liability, but the courts found in the favour of those who had bought the product in good faith.

The weblink leads to a short article that looks at the lack of even basic risk management at the time. The consequences were that Hoover eventually spent '£48 million' in response to thousands of irate customers ('Hoover's free flights fiasco recalled', *Source*: http://news.bbc.co.uk/1/hi/business/3704669.stm).

Ask yourselves the following:

What went wrong?
Why?

ACTIVITY 9.1

Scan the marketing press and begin your file of examples in this area. It is important to try to analyse these examples from a risk management perspective. Remember that a 'smart man learns from his own mistakes, a wise man learns from others mistakes, a fool does neither' (Lam, 2003).

CASE EXAMPLE – HBOS

Risk managers at HBOS were discouraged from challenging business decisions. Anthony Smith said that the risk group's culture changed in 2005 after his boss Paul Moore was replaced by someone with no experience of risk or regulation.

'There was definitely a dumbing down of the risk function and challenging the business... was not welcome', he said.

The bank said Mr Smith was a 'junior employee' and the new director of risk was a 'senior banker'. How HBOS was run has come under question in recent weeks after Paul Moore, former head of regulatory risk, alleged that he was sacked after warning the bank about excessive risk taking. HBOS denied the allegations and pointed out that an inquiry had concluded they were 'unfounded', but the publicity led to the resignation of former HBOS chief executive Sir James Crosby as deputy chairman of the City watchdog the Financial Services Authority (FSA).

Anthony Smith, who worked for the banking group as a manager until late 2005, told the BBC that Mr. Moore's successor as the risk director Jo Dawson knew nothing about risk or regulation, a claim the bank denies.

Mr. Smith described an occasion when Jo Dawson was asked to speak at a dinner attended by FSA chief executive John Tiner and other senior regulators.

'She didn't want to look foolish at that meeting, obviously, so I was asked to prepare a four page bullet-point summary of regulation for her', he said.

Mr. Smith received an email thanking him for the note, saying that Ms. Dawson 'found it very easy to understand and didn't need any extra explanations'.

'I thought it was a little bit strange for somebody in that position, to be on the board advising them about risk who has no knowledge at all about risk and regulation', Mr. Smith said.

However, a spokesperson for Lloyds Banking Group, which took over HBOS last year, said: 'Jo Dawson is a very experienced and senior banker with more than 20 years experience in the industry. She took her role as risk director very seriously indeed'.

An investigation by KPMG also supported the appointment of the new risk director.

The culture in the risk group changed following the departure of Paul Moore, according to Mr. Smith, with steps taken to prevent them challenging the way the bank was being run. He said they introduced relationship managers who had to communicate with the rest of the organisation 'in a friendly way so as not to upset the business'.

Mr. Smith gave the example of an occasion when he had reported compliance problems after carrying out a review of the advertising of HBOS's financial products.

He said he was told that he could not write a report in such a direct fashion.

'The problems took about six to 10 months to resolve. When really we could have sorted them out straight away'.

'We were constantly being pushed back and constantly being told that things had to be put in a way that wasn't going to upset the business-basically that wasn't going to stand in the way of the sales culture at the time'.

The discussion of the risks taken by HBOS has been particularly pertinent since Friday last week, when Lloyds Banking Group, which now owns HBOS, announced that its acquisition would be announcing full-year losses of about £10 billion.

Source: BBC, 2009

How could this have been managed more effectively?
What lessons can be learned?

What is Risk?

Chapman and Ward tell us that 'all projects involve risk – the zero risk project is not worth pursuing...some degree of risk is likely to yield a more

FIGURE 9.1

Risk and return

Source: Lam, 2003

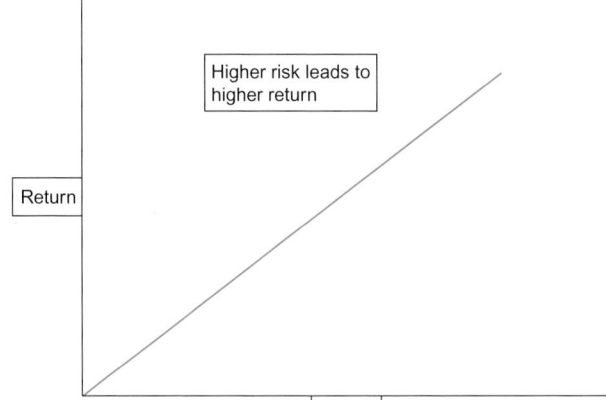

desirable and appropriate level of return for the resources committed to the venture' (Chapman and Ward, 2003).

Risk can be defined simply as hazard, or the possibility of experience loss or harm.

Whilst this is common sense, it is clear that the level of risk and the nature of the rewards from risk avoidance or management will vary according to the project that is being undertaken. There are degrees of risk, and the ability or willingness to experience risk occurs often in relation to the reward that is available from exposing ourselves to that risk.

The risk attached to crossing the road is far less than a tightrope walker using a tightrope to cross the same road. Equally, if I was crossing the road to ask a stranger for the time, I would be less inclined to take that risk than if the person on the opposite side were a friend I had not seen for ages and who owed me money!

Lam (2003) shows that this can be expressed graphically in a simplistic form (Figure 9.1).

However, this is an oversimplification of the facts; there is always an optimal balance between the rate of return and risk. The representation below comes closer to the truth (Figure 9.2).

So, a clear principle is established early on. We need to assess risk and weigh up the impact of that risk in accordance with the likelihood of the perceived risk being actually experienced and in the light of the potential rewards available to us.

Lewis (2007) defines risk simply as 'anything that can go wrong with a project'.

Gardiner in his book on project management contrasts between two definitions; the first his own:

'An event with an undesirable outcome for the project that may happen sometime in the future' (Gardiner, 2005).

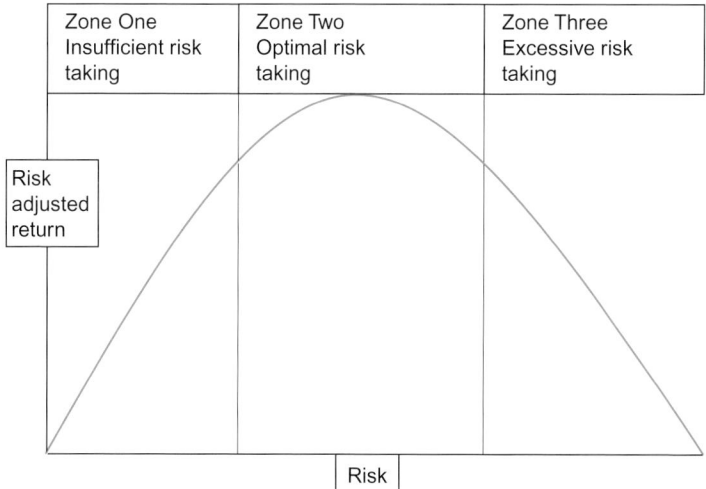

Zone One Insufficient risk taking	Zone Two Optimal risk taking	Zone Three Excessive risk taking

Risk
adjusted
return

Risk

FIGURE 9.2

Risk and relative return
Source: Lam, 2003

He contrasts this with the Project Management Institute's definition that describes risk as:

'An uncertain event or condition that, if it occurs, has a positive or negative effect on a project outcome' (PMI, 2000 cited in Gardiner, 2005).

This can be set against the Association of Project Management's (APM) definition of risk as 'an uncertain event or set of circumstances that should it occur will have an effect on the achievement of the projects objectives' (APM, 2007 cited in Chapman and Ward, 2003).

RISKS vs. THREATS

Earlier in the workbook, you will have seen the use of SWOT. Lewis reminds us that there is a difference between Threats and Risk. 'Risks are things that can happen without having any deliberate intention to cause harm' (Lewis, 2007). This means that threats are something that is done by a competitor to interfere actively to compromise your business goals. Risks may include acts of God, fire, flood etc., accidents, financial problems, staffing issues, the impact of technology breakthroughs or the output of political change.

PERSPECTIVES ON RISK

The perception of risk varies according to organisational culture and the markets in which they operate. In the last six months, we have seen companies like RBS and HBOS reaping the effects of a bullish approach to the identification and acceptance of risk. The commentary has focused on the failure of risk management in these organisations in comparison to other companies operating in the same sector.

To be fair, these organisations were responding to a variety of factors operating in the market and with the benefit of hindsight, it is easy to say that they were reckless. Six months ago however, the same commentators were praising the strategies pursued by these companies and marking their share prices up to record levels.

The process of identifying, assessing and managing risk works at many levels and risk can be experienced at any level within the organisation.

STRATEGIC RISKS

Strategic risks are those relating to projects concerning the strategic orientation of the organisation within its environment, and are concerned with the management of the long-term direction of the organisation.

You should be familiar with the Ansoff matrix. At the heart of this strategic tool is an assessment of the risk relating to strategic options (Table 9.1).

The evidence here is that for one of the most basic tools for determining the marketing strategy, risk is at its heart. However, the strategic management of risk is not often seen as a key marketing skill. A strategic approach to risk should have the following impacts:

- Speed up the process of delivery of new marketing initiatives.
- Enhance upside value of marketing projects.
- Provide a case for budget allocation.
- Improve the process and output of planning at strategic, tactical and operational level.

OPERATIONAL RISKS

These risks relate to the day-to-day implementation of marketing projects; they may relate to a failure to manage the project effectively, individual management issues and failure to manage supply chains or data systems.

Table 9.1   Risk and the Ansoff matrix

	Existing markets	New markets
Existing products	Market Penetration Lower risk 1	Market Development Higher risk 4
New products	Product Development Higher risk 2	Diversification Highest risk 16

Source: Ansoff Growth Matrix, 1954.

FINANCIAL RISKS

Risks relating to the financial management of projects, changes in interest rates, exchange rate fluctuations, and risks relating to credit or cash flow.

KNOWLEDGE RISKS

The ability to capture and act on knowledge relating to the successful delivery of the project is central to its successful implementation.

COMPLIANCE RISKS

Risks may relate to compliance with regulatory framework, codes of conduct or legislation.

PROJECT-BASED RISKS

There is a range of risks relating to the planning process itself.

RISKS AND THE MARKETING PLAN

The creation, execution, control and monitoring of the marketing plan has the characteristics of a major project. Risk can be identified, assessed and controlled at all stages of the plan, from the analysis of the environment, its impact on objective setting, the development of strategy and the tactical mix around this to the key areas of monitoring control and contingency. The ability to manage this process is a core competence for marketing managers.

Typically, the planning process is managed to deliver value to customers who give us something in return, often money, but occasionally we are looking for a change in behaviour or attitudes. For example, governments spend money on marketing to get people to live a healthier lifestyle, to pay their taxes and drive safely.

Planning reconciles the interests of the customer base, the activities of the management responsible for execution of the plan and delivers the desired output from this interaction, typically expressed in terms of profit or value creation.

These phrases may bring to mind the definition of marketing by the CIM and the American Marketing Association.

'Marketing is the management process responsible for identifying, anticipating and satisfying customer requirements profitably' (CIM, 2005).

The CIM describes marketing as both a concept dedicated to meeting customer requirements and a range of techniques, which enables the company to determine those requirements and ensure that they are met. The output of these processes is a mutually satisfying exchange of value. This is better expressed in the AMA's (American Marketing Association's) definition below.

'Marketing is the activity, set of institutions, and processes for creating, communicating, delivering, and exchanging offerings that have value for customers, clients, partners, and society at large'.

The fact that risk is experienced at many different levels as we have seen above means that the classification of risk under those related to customer, management and the outcome in terms of profit is useful.

Risks affecting the interaction with customers can be experienced at all levels within the planning process. At a strategic level, they may be related to the effort to exploit new markets or develop new products, rebranding or repositioning the brand. At a tactical level, it may relate to an element of the mix, for example, a failure in service delivery or inappropriate use of data.

The assessment of risk within the plan and the implementation of contingency plans are assessed later in this module. Clearly, changes to the marketing plan in order to avoid or mitigate risk place demands on the resource base of the business. This may mean that financial resources are needed to mitigate the effects of risk or that different management skills are required to manage the issues that emerge.

Risk assessment should also include an assessment of the competencies of the management team required to deliver the plan.

Ultimately, the impact of risk is assessed in a commercial environment in terms of impact on the bottom line.

As the Financial Reporting Council (FRC) states:

'A company's objectives, its internal organisation and the environment in which it operates are continually evolving and, as a result, the risks it faces are continually changing. A sound system of internal control therefore depends on a thorough and regular evaluation of the nature and extent of the risks to which the company is exposed. Since profits are, in part, the reward for successful risk-taking in business, the purpose of internal control is to help manage and control risk appropriately rather than to eliminate it' (FRC, 2005).

We will see later the techniques for assessing the profit impact of risk assessment and the impact of management and mitigation.

Risk can therefore be assessed at many different levels and because of organisational complexity, a range of services exist to help the risk assessment planning process. For example, Price Waterhouse Cooper has a bespoke system for providing risk analysis for its customers.

CASE EXAMPLE – Institute of Chartered Accountants in England & Wales

Risks according to the faculty of finance and management of The Institute of Chartered Accountants in England & Wales (ICAEW):

1. Strategic risks arise from being in a particular industry and geographical area.
2. Operational risks arise from the various operational and administrative procedures that the business uses to implement its strategy.
3. Financial risks arise from the financial structure of the business, from transactions with third parties and from the financial systems in place.
4. Compliance risks derive from the necessity to ensure compliance with laws, regulations and other less-formal societal expectations that, if infringed, can damage a company.
5. Health and safety risks are sometimes straightforward and can be considered as a subset of compliance or operational risk, but in many industries (e.g. transport), health and safety are key areas that require major resources and concentration.
6. Environmental risks can be relatively routine and covered under compliance, but in many businesses (and in an increasingly large number), they are a major area requiring separate consideration.

Source: The Faculty of Finance and Management of the Institute of Chartered Accountants in England & Wales, 2002

CASE EXAMPLE – PWC

Risk Assessment and PWC

PWC's web-enabled survey solution offers clients the benefits of polling employees confidentially and provides feedback in the following areas considered to be the Key Attributes of Effective Risk Management:

Leadership and Strategy – how well does leadership demonstrate ethics and values and communicate its mission and objectives throughout the organisation. It focuses on leadership policy and procedures, top–down alignment of strategy, done at the top, and personal ethics.

Accountability and Reinforcement – the ability of the organisation to assign individual accountability within the organisation and the ability to measure and reward performances.

People and Communication – how well does the organisation share knowledge and information and promote and develop employee competence: through training, setting performance indicators, the use of incentives and disciplinary policies.

Risk Management and Infrastructure – the ability of the organisation to assess and measure risk and establish processes and controls to mitigate that risk. This would involve output assessing information quality, top–down communications, cross-process communications, process reliability, control efficiency and effectiveness, system access and security, risk assessment practices, risk tools and processes.

The confidential feedback harvested by the RCS (Risk Culture Survey) process allows management to make informed decisions about cultural changes integral to creating an environment that is conducive to ethical behaviour and honest communication, and allows for the proactive management of risks to avoid surprises.

What are the typical issues identified by the Risk Culture Survey?

The Risk Culture Survey is best used to provide in-depth information on the effectiveness of an existing risk management programme or to quantify the understanding of risk within an organisation in order to establish the foundation for a risk management initiative. The following are examples of issues identified by the Risk Culture Survey for clients:

1. Awareness and understanding of business risks throughout the enterprise
2. Understanding of risks is inconsistent or non-existent
3. Lack of emphasis of risk management and control by management
4. Inconsistent direction by management
5. The impact of change
6. Controls lacking or not working
7. Lack of training on risk management
8. Ability to link business risk and control perspectives at the 'top' to the perspectives of people on the front lines
9. Messengers of bad news are not well received by management
10. Lack of individual accountability for objectives
11. Misalignment of objectives from corporate to business units
12. Lack of understanding of policies
13. Identification of internal audit approach focused more on 'gotcha's' than on providing value
14. Ability to operationalise risk management strategies through action plans that align key business initiatives with systemic risks
15. Integrate the consideration of risks in process redesign projects
16. Explicit identification and analysis of risks in the design and monitoring of asset management plans
17. No performance measures
18. Improper ethics and compliance practices identified
19. Sales practices
20. No disciplinary action for professional misconduct
21. Improprieties
22. Direct input on how well people strategy is working
23. Turnover and its impact to achieving objectives
24. Inconsistent treatment of employees by management
25. Lack of skilled resources
26. Lack of consistent application of incentive programmes
27. Incentives focus only on short-term objectives
28. Lack timely completion of performance reviews
29. No performance review process in place
30. What are the possible next steps that a company can take after conducting a Risk Culture Survey for the company?
31. Some examples of additional initiatives undertaken, as a result of issues identified through the Risk Culture Survey, to enhance existing risk management programmes:
32. Hiring & exit interview/turnover processes & management restructuring
33. Facilitated Control Assessment Session(s) to identify root causes
34. Enterprise Risk Assessment
35. Risk Management Training
36. IT Controls Assessment
37. Executive Communications Strategy
38. Assessment of Internal Audit Function & Approach
39. Structuring of the Chief Risk Officer Function

Source: PWC, 2009

SUMMARY

In this chapter, we concentrated on the very important aspect for organisations to be aware of risk. We looked at the core elements involved in the identification of risk and the varying and different types and nature of risk.

CHAPTER 10

Risk Assessment and Evaluation

INTRODUCTION

Whatever the risks an organisation experiences, they all have certain characteristics:

- They exist in the future and we can moderate the future effect by analysis of past events.
- They are wholly or partially unknown.
- They are not constant in that they change over time and in relation to context.
- Their impact may be managed, moderated, removed or controlled.
- They are ubiquitous to all projects.

Risk management has become an important area for marketing. The nature of marketing projects as we have seen has changed and many of these involve a very high degree of resource commitment, for example, the development of a CRM (Customer Relationship Management) system or the development of international operations. The need for marketing to be accountable at all times has become paramount, and calculating and managing exposure to risk and the potential returns on activity is a characteristic of good marketing management.

The management of risk has been described as the new Total Quality Management (TQM), and it is true to say that the management of risk and the attendant benefits from the effective delivery of risk management is a key criterion against which effective marketing management is assessed.

The management of risk is a key driver of financial performance and can drive shareholder and stakeholder value. In doing so, it creates opportunities and stability for all those involved in the organisation.

The Risk Management Process

Gardiner (2005) says that risk planning can be divided into two phases: risk assessment and risk control.

Risk assessment includes:

- Risk identification
- Risk analysis
- Risk prioritisation

Risk control includes:

- Risk response planning
- Risk resolution
- Risk monitoring and reporting

Other frameworks are more complex, but they all involve the following stages:

- The monitoring, identification of risk or risk audit
- The evaluation, classification and assessment of risk
  a. Qualitative assessment
  b. Quantitative assessment
- The management or treatment of risk
- Risk review and reporting

Identifying Sources of Risk, The Risk Auditing Process

Where does risk come from? There are several useful frameworks that can be applied to the identification and assessment of risk in marketing projects. Chapman and Ward use the 6Ws framework as a starting point to help the identification of risks (Table 10.1).

Each of these aspects fits within the broader project management process that we have seen earlier in the workbook. At its simplest, the three-stage SHAMPU model:

Shape
Harness and
Manage

Table 10.1	Chapman and Ward 6Ws framework
Who:	Are the parties involved?
What:	What are the parties interested in?
Wherewithal:	What resources are required?
Why:	What do they want to achieve?
Which way:	How is it to be done?
When:	When does it have to be done?

Source: Chapman and Ward, 2003

highlights risks of different types with different degrees of severity and with a different range of potential outcomes (Figure 10.1).

A risk plan will take in to account the following risk categories:

1. Risks that exist and are controlled and managed within the project being undertaken

2. Risks in the external environment, whose resolution depends on decisions being taken that rest largely outside our immediate control

3. Risks that are wholly uncontrollable such as natural disasters

Conception	Level of project definition Definition of appropriate performance objectives Stakeholder expectations
Design	Novelty of design and technology
Plan the execution strategically	Regulatory constraints Milestone management and concurrency of activities Capturing dependency relationships Errors and omissions
Allocate resources tactically	Adequate resource estimates
	Estimating resources required Defining responsibilities Defining contractual terms and conditions Selection of capable participants
Execute production	Exercise adequate co-ordination and control Determine level and scope of control systems Ensuring effective communications between partners Ensure effective leadership Ensure continuity in personnel and responsibilities
Deliver the project	Adequate testing Adequate training Managing stakeholder expectations Obtaining licences
Review the process	Capturing corporate knowledge Learning Understanding success
Support the ongoing implementation	Organise Identity liabilities Manage expectations

FIGURE 10.1

Uncertainty and risk at each stage of the project life cycle
Source: Chapman and Ward, 2003

Table 10.2	The Ernst and Young strategic risk radar: the top ten strategic threats for global business in 2008

Macro threats
Energy shocks
Global financial shocks

Operational threats
Poor execution of strategic decisions
Cost inflation

Sector threats
Inability to respond to sector consolidation or transition
Regulatory and compliance risk
Inability to capitalise on emerging market opportunity
Ageing consumers and workforce
Radical greening
Consumer demand shifts

The next five
War for talent
Pandemic
Private equity rise
Inability to innovate
China setback

Source: Ernst and Young, 2008

In 2008, Ernst and Young published a survey on sources of risk. They consolidated these into strategic risk radar, and this is summarised in Table 10.2.

Of course, this table focuses on the potential sources of risk for larger businesses; however, some of the categories are relevant for all businesses including SMEs.

Risks that relate to marketing projects may include the above and perhaps some of the following:

PEST factors

1. Legal and political – regime change, EU legislation, new tax laws etc.

2. Risks relating to finance and money – overspending, increase in the cost of money, failure to secure additional funding, credit crunch, falling asset values.

3. Technical risks include redundant technology as well as technological advances.

4. Risks relating to changes in the consumer – social changes, increase in divorce and lone parents, an ageing population, increasing numbers on higher and further education, end of the job for life culture.

5. Risks relating to the performance of individuals involved in the project – illness or other incapacity, skills base etc.

Other factors

1. Business impact and benefits, for example, the strategic impact of projects, the level of stakeholder support and engagement.

2. Risks may relate to standing or reputation, a loss of confidence in the organisation may seriously damage our ability to meet project objectives.

3. Risks that relate to the organisation itself and the impact of the project on the organisation, which departments are involved, how well do they communicate, the level of political conflict and cultural issues.

4. Systems and procedural failures, database crash or the failure of internal audit and reporting systems, logistical issues.

5. Risks inherent in the project itself, running overtime, poor-quality outputs, staff skills base, stakeholder attitudes.

6. Testing, compliance and standards issues.

7. Acts of God or natural disasters like floods, fires etc.

8. Competitive threats, new entrants or supplier dominance may have a significant impact.

Identification of these risks is obviously project specific and the list above is not exhaustive. Once the risks have been identified, it is then necessary to evaluate the risks, and the first stage is to establish where and if they apply. Is the project particularly vulnerable to any of the risks identified and if so at what stage and to what extent? The precise evaluation and quantification of risk comes later in this section.

ACTIVITY 10.1

For any particular project you are familiar with, use one of the frameworks above to identify the risks that may affect the ability to complete the project.

Techniques for Risk Identification

The process of risk identification should follow a set procedure in a proactive way and be as comprehensive as possible.

All relevant sources should be considered.
These may include:

- Past project files
- Project planning documentation
- Risk checklists
- Feasibility reports
- Expert interviews
- Trade-off analyses

The major techniques for risk identification are listed below.

- Team briefings or risk clinics/Brainstorming
- SWOT analyses
- Cause and effect diagrams
- Risk concepts mapping

Team Briefings or Risk Clinics/Brainstorming

Lewis in his book on project management talks about the technique he advises clients to use when trying to identify the risk attached to certain projects:

'I have them brainstorm a list of potential pitfalls and record them on a flip chart with no discussion or evaluation...I simply ask, What could go wrong that could impact schedule, cost performance or scope in the project' (Lewis, 2007)?

The rules for successful brainstorming are as follows:

- Facilitators should be chosen carefully
- All relevant parties should attend, this may mean 5–30 participants
- Have clear objectives without narrowing or biasing the scope of enquiry
- No idea is wrong; leaders should create a sense that everything is on the table and be inclusive
- Never judge at this stage
- Quantity is a virtue at this stage
- Build on discussions, make links and try to reach a position where every aspect of the issue has been explored
- Have an independent scribe to record the discussion
- Create a good physical environment – consider the room layout, a circle may be appropriate, heat light and refreshments

Even at this stage, it may be helpful to begin the process of risk classification. Lock (2003) suggests that risks might be usefully grouped under the following headings:

1. Risks most likely to occur at the start of the process
2. Risks most likely to occur during execution

3. Risk that may affect the final stages of the project
4. Risks that occur on implementation
5. Risks that may affect the project at any stage

SWOT Analyses

So, a mere identification of risk is not sufficient. Identification includes the process of categorisation and prioritising. SWOT or TOWS should be techniques with which you are familiar. Strengths Weaknesses Opportunities and Threats analysis is a well used and trusted device for helping us cope with complex situations quickly.

Its strength is that it considers internal drivers under strengths and weaknesses and the external factors under opportunity and threat.

The process however needs careful consideration and there are a variety of ways to make the SWOT work effectively; we will consider some of these in more detail later on.

The SWOT must be based on accurate and realistic data. We must consider honestly the internal aspects of the SWOT; it may be tempting to overestimate senior management capabilities for political purposes. We can prioritise within the analysis; this involves simply ranking factors from one to ten according to their perceived importance. It can be based on some quantitative analysis or on judgement or a combination of the two, and we will explore quantitative analysis later.

The SWOT can be oriented around Opportunities. Therefore, if the organisation is driven by the opportunities that exist for it, how can we manage our strengths, counter weaknesses and deal with the threats that may prevent us from exploiting these opportunities? The nature of the opportunities can also be considered in terms of attractiveness and fit with the organisation's capabilities. Where appropriate, combine the SWOT with other frameworks, for example asset-based analysis and competency analysis.

Cause and Effect Diagrams

Cause and effect diagrams are a useful way of looking at the range of risks and beginning to classify their potential impacts on the organisations concerned (Figure 10.2).

The most common form of cause and effect diagram is the Ishikawa fishbone analysis. The diagram above could be presented in this way, with ever-increasing levels of analysis. For example, the Poor Management Information entry might have its own subsidiary causes, but ultimately, this produces a complex diagram (Figure 10.3).

The strengths of the fishbone analysis are that they represent graphically and accessibly the drivers of risk.

FIGURE 10.2

A cut down cause and effect diagram

Possible causes		Effect
Human Skills base lacking Skills shortage Limited training	**Organisational** No senior involvement in decision-making Interdepartmental conflict Poor briefing of external suppliers	Project overspend
Operational Failure to communicate Poor project management control systems Diverse teams	**Financial** Inadequate financial controls Poor management information	

FIGURE 10.3

Ishikawa fishbone diagram

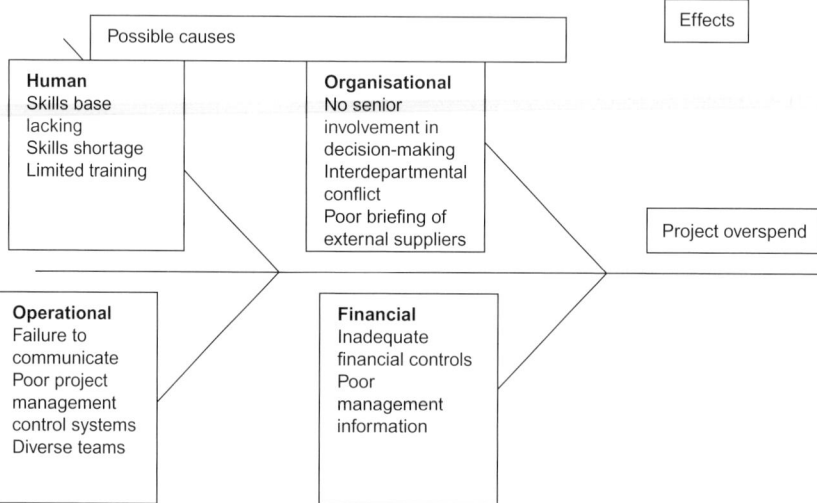

The weakness is that they look at the output first and then try to understand what has caused this. In reality, the management of risk implies that we start by trying to isolate and manage the causes.

Risk Concepts Maps

A risk concept map is defined as 'a flow diagram designed to show in one picture the total risk scenario of a project or programme' (Bartlett, 2002 cited in Gardiner, 2005).

A risk concept map will contain key risk drivers, which create individual risk situations and associated impacts. Assumptions and reactions can also be included.

For example, the launch of a new international database system may include the following:

The risk driver might be national cultural differences
The risk situation might be inconsistencies in data capture and
    maintenance

The impacts may be:

Marketing managers lose faith in the system
Replica systems set up
Data protection rules are broken

Risk Evaluation

Once risks have been identified, then they need to be analysed for their impact, and there is a range of tools to help us with this task.

We are trying to predict the likelihood of the risk being experienced and the impact of risk on the project schedule costs and performance and other resources required to manage this risk. This can involve both qualitative and quantitative methods. There is some debate about the relative importance of these approaches and their use depends on the nature of the project and the nature of the risks.

Some risks are harder to quantify than others. For example, the impact of cost overruns maybe easier to measure than the lack of commitment to a project from senior staff.

The key objective is to help us prioritise risk and to allocate resources appropriate to the mitigation of that risk.

Risk Assessment Matrices

One of the simplest techniques to achieve the basic aim of risk management is to develop a risk assessment matrix.

This simply assigns a score to the probability of the risk being experienced and the impact of this risk (Table 10.3).

Each risk is put in one of the nine boxes; this is best done as a team as individuals will perceive risk differently.

The output helps assess the vulnerability of the project to risk. A high-risk project may have one or more risks evaluated at 9; a lower-risk project may have the majority of risks at fewer than 3.

The output of this is a simple formula:

$$\text{risk exposure} = \text{probability of risk} \times \text{impact}.$$

Table 10.3		Risk assessment matrix		
Probability		**Impact**		
		Low 1	**Medium 2**	**High 3**
Low	1	1	2	3
Medium	2	2	4	6
High	3	3	6	9

Risk Quantification

There are a number of quantification techniques for risk assessment. The most commonly used are:

- Expected value
- Sensitivity analysis
- Monte Carlo simulations
- Failure mode effect criticality analysis
- PERT

Expected Value

This is a technique for helping us assess the output of a project and mitigating this against the risk or likelihood of occurrence.

If the development of a new product line has a 66% chance of generating a profit of 10 million, then the expected value is $0.66 \times £10,000,000$ or £660,000.

Expected value can be used to allocate resources to alternative projects taking into account the level of return and the impact of risk in terms of the likelihood of successful delivery of the project.

Sensitivity Analysis

This analysis allows us to evaluate the impact of a range of risks and the financial impact of these risks, for example, in the context of the cost of inputs into the project, which are likely to change over time. Over the last few years, for example, we have seen major changes in the price of energy inputs and raw materials.

An expected value of the main inputs into the project is calculated and a sensitivity analysis is applied for example at ±15% (Table 10.4). In the example below, we have the following figures:

Revenue	£1,000,000
Materials	£400,000
Labour	£100,000
Overheads	£200,000 constant

Table 10.4	Sensitivity analysis		
	−15%	**Materials expected**	**+15%**
−15%	1,000,000	1,000,000	1,000,000
	340,000	400,000	460,000
	85,000	85,000	85,000
	200,000	200,000	200,000
	375,000	**315,000**	**255,000**
Labour expected	1,000,000	1,000,000	1,000,000
	340,000	400,000	460,000
	100,000	100,000	100,000
	200,000	200,000	200,000
	360,000	**300,000**	**240,000**
+15%	1,000,000	1,000,000	1,000,000
	340,000	400,000	460,000
	115,000	115,000	115,000
	200,000	200,000	200,000
	345,000	**285,000**	**225,000**

Table 10.5	Failure, mode and effect matrix				
	Risk item	**Failure mode**	**Cause of failure**	**Effect**	**Remedial action**
1	Product	Product contamination	Faulty cleaning Contaminated ingredients	Illness Litigation Reputation Brand values Product withdrawal	Institute crisis planning
2	Etc				
3					

Monte Carlo Simulation

This is a computer-generated model providing data on a range of variables with different values and distribution, for example costs timings, input costs and shows the impact on a range of outputs, for example financial outputs.

It is available on Excel as well as in many bespoke project management software products. It is linked to Project Evaluation and Review Techniques (PERT) in that it deals with a range of possible outcomes. A consideration of the PERT technique follows below.

Failure, Mode and Effect Analysis

This is a useful approach as it takes into account all possible risks and also tries to outline their possible effects. This may be quantified although often no priority is given to the risks described (Table 10.5).

	Risk item	Failure mode	Cause of failure	Effect	Remedial action	Probability	Impact	Detection	Total
	Table 10.6	Failure mode and effect criticality matrix							
1	Product	Product contamination	Faulty cleaning Contaminated ingredients	Illness Litigation Reputation Brand values Product withdrawal	Institute crisis planning	1	5	3	9
2	Etc								
3									

The failure, mode and effect analysis may be quantified. Table 10.6 illustrates how this is done with a score entered for the key risk variables identified by the project team. Again, there may be many risk items considered within the table.

PERT

Project Evaluation and Review Techniques (PERT) deal with the fact that the estimated time for completion on any project will almost certainly vary. Instead of taking one value, the techniques deals with three values:

1. O = Optimistic time, if conditions are perfect, the time taken to complete a task
2. M = Most probable time under expected conditions
3. P = Pessimistic time if we experience some of the things that could go wrong

The distribution of these figures will vary; there may be little difference or a large difference in the range of figures. However, we cause the figures entered to work out the expected time that a task will take.

For example, look at the following figures:

O = 3
M = 5
P = 7

Using the formula, we arrive at the expected time (e):

E = [o + 4m + p]/6

Therefore, for this activity, the expected time is:

[3 + [4 × 5] + 7]/6 = 5

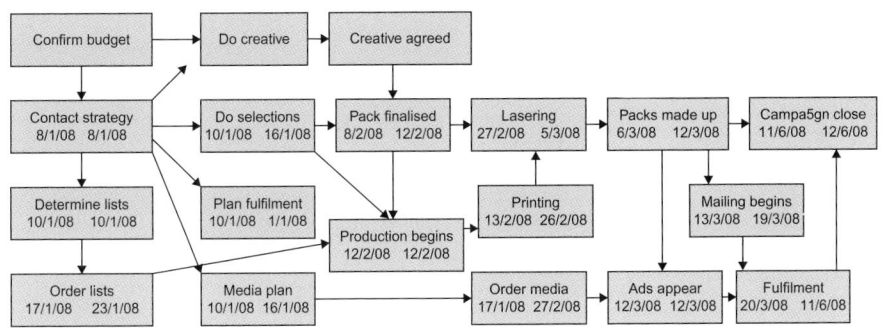

FIGURE 10.4
*A PERT-based chart for the
production of mailing
Source: © The IDM, 2009
with permission*

Table 10.7	Probability of occurrence	
Probability	**Possible rate of occurrence**	**Score**
Very high	>1 in 2	10
	1 in 3	9
High	1 in 8	8
	1 in 20	7
Moderate	1 in 80	6
	1 in 400	5
	1 in 2,000	4
Low	1 in 15,000	3
	1 in 150,000	2
Remote	<1 in 1,500,000	1

Source: Lewis, 2008

We can do this for any number of tasks and work out the expected time of the entire project in this way.

In reality, for most large projects, the computer will complete the analysis (Figure 10.4).

Probability Analyses

As we have seen that the identification of risk is only one small part of the risk management process, what concerns the marketing project manager is the probability of that risk being experienced. This can be combined with a measure of the severity of the impact and our ability to detect this risk to produce an overall risk probability score. Lewis (2007) suggests the use of a logarithmic scale to estimate the probability of occurrence (Table 10.7).

The second area to consider is the impact of the risk being experienced (Table 10.8).

Table 10.8	Assessing impact	
Effect	**Impact**	**Score**
Severe unforeseen	Terminal	10
Severe foreseen	Severe implication	9
Very serious	Delay and/or financial repercussion	8
Serious	Significant impact; project delivered but significantly below expectations	7
Moderate	Noticeable impact on desired outputs	6
Low	Limited impact to deliverables	5
Very low	Very limited impact	4
Insignificant	Minor impact	3
Very insignificant	Little or no impact	2
Zero	No impact	1

Table 10.9	Capability of detection
Detectable	**Score**
Unknown	10
Very unlikely	9
Unlikely	8
Very low	7
Low	6
Moderate	5
Reasonably high	4
High	3
Very high	2
More or less certain	1

Clear probability is of little consequence on its own. If an event is likely to occur but is of limited consequence, then it may be ignored.

The final area to consider is the ability to detect the risk before its impact is felt (Table 10.9).

Again, this can be given a score.

These elements can be combined into a final risk analysis schedule of the project. The outcome of this process is a risk probability number for the risk attached to any specific projects. We can see this for selected risk relating to an industry conference (Table 10.10).

Table 10.10	Selected risk analysis, industry conference			
Risk	**P**	**I**	**D**	**Risk probability number**
Power fails	3	10	8	240
Projection fails	5	8	3	120
Loss of key speaker	3	8	5	120

Scenario Planning

It is a technique that can be used to determine the risks and opportunities relating particularly to the long-term strategic direction of the organisation. It is a complex process and normally involves experts from a range of related areas or departments within the organisation. The use of external consultants is common.

In her book *Scenario Planning*, Gill Ringland (2006) identified several outputs of the scenario planning process.

- Erste Allgemeine Versicherung, the Austrian insurance company, anticipated the fall of the Berlin Wall and entered new markets in central Europe.
- KRONE, the wiring and cable supplier, developed 200 new product ideas.
- Unilever decided on marketing strategies for Russia and Poland.
- United Distillers (now Diageo) set market strategies for India, South Africa and Turkey.
- Electrolux spotted new consumer markets.

Shell's scenario planning is world renowned, as they seek to manage the volatility around the politics of global energy management.

The process is as follows:

- Define the scenario
- Identify the risks relating to that scenario
- Create a plan to identify early warning indicators and identify management responses
- Communicate this plan to all parties involved in resolving the scenario
- Review regularly

Event Tree Analysis

Event trees are diagrammatic representations of the range of outputs that occur in response to any event, including risks that can happen within a project. With the increase in the number of outputs, the diagram grows to look like the branches of a tree.

FIGURE 10.5
Event tree

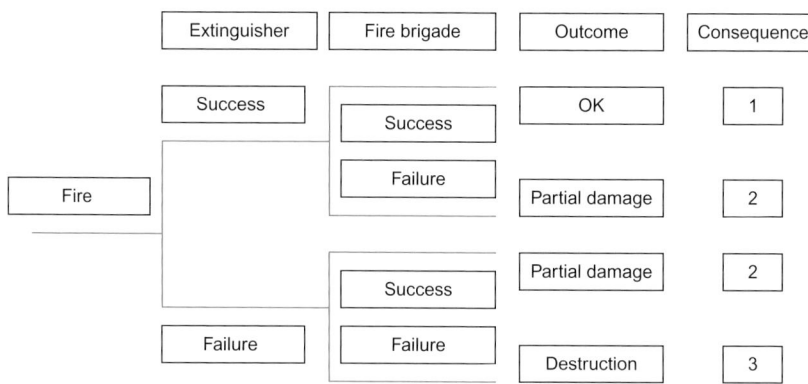

We always start with what is known as the initiating event, and the event tree helps us to analyse the potential results of a range of alternative reactions to this initial event, whether they successfully resolve the issues or exacerbate it.

The example below draws on the risk of fire (Figure 10.5). There are two systems that are designed to deal with this: a fire extinguishing system and an automated call to the fire brigade.

It is possible to enhance this process through a variety of additional activities. For example, we can add probabilities impact assessment scores and values to outcomes to create a graphical representation of the projects and related picture of the risks and opportunities (Figure 10.6).

Assumptions Analysis

Assumptions analysis is an important technique. It is designed to ensure that the risks that are inherent in making assumptions around project plans.

Interested parties and team members should list the assumptions that have been made and built into the project planning process. For each of these assumptions, risks should be identified on the basis of potential mistakes or incorrect application of the assumption. The team should assess the assumption for validity and if it is believed that the assumption is not valid, it should be reassessed. This process is ongoing through the project planning process.

CASE EXAMPLE – Tots to Travel

Here's how risk assessment helped my business
Wendy Shand started her online business Tots to Travel, which promotes and books holiday accommodation that is as safe as possible for children, in 2006. Carrying out risk assessments on each holiday home is vital to protect the brand, but Wendy realises that assessing risks in other parts of the business is key, too. Here, she explains how it has helped her firm.

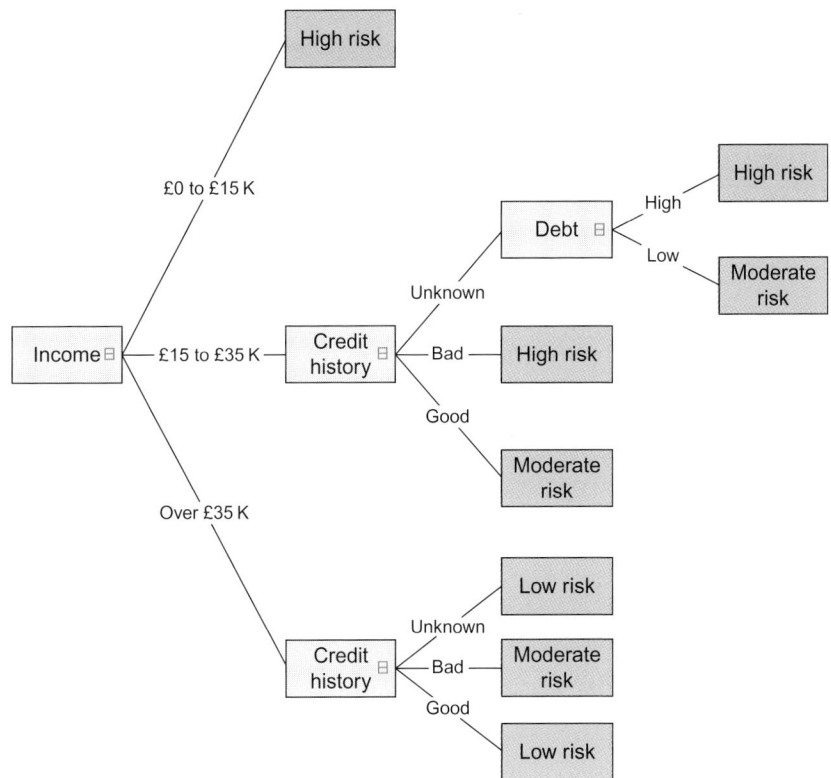

FIGURE 10.6
Risk tree
*Source: Smartdraw,
www.SmartDraw.com*

What I Did
'Tots to Travel resulted from a holiday with our children in France. We rented a house that was lovely, but it didn't have things we took for granted at home such as stair gates. I felt I could do better'.

Risk Assessing Properties
'Tots to Travel is currently focused on France and Italy, with Spain, Portugal, Turkey and the UK being added shortly. We risk assess in terms of safety and we insist on vetting properties in person because there is a lot tied up in a holiday – not just financially, but emotionally as well'.

'We have a rigorous list of safety criteria that we worked out with the Child Accident Prevention Trust. Some houses in France don't have banisters, for example. If the owner is not prepared to make changes to meet our requirements, then it's not in our best interest to go and visit that property'.

'Careful risk assessment means we are able to make better decisions – for example, in France there is strict legislation that says pools need to be alarmed, fenced or covered – so we do not visit properties unless they meet these criteria. Elsewhere where legislation is not so tight, we have to look more creatively at pool security. Not getting it right is a risk to our brand, dealing with complaints is time-consuming and emotionally draining, and an accident would be even worse'.

'Spending time assessing our potential risks has also put us ahead of the competition. It's good for business, as naturally parents want to go on a holiday where their children are as safe as possible – so they come to us'.

Assessing Other Risks
'Without risk assessment, an accident, litigation case or the loss of all our data could blind-side us-financially, emotionally and practically'.

'We've considered various risks-things like cashflow, what happens if a member of staff leaves, if someone decides to sue us, or if our computers go down. We have put in place a basic, written, action plan for each so that if they happen it is not so much of a crisis'.

'If our website and database were lost, it would represent three years' worth of work. Our technology is so vital that our systems are backed up three times. We have a back-up server in the house and one in the office, and as a third precaution there is a daily back-up in a vault in Canary Wharf'.

'We also look carefully at our insurance policies annually, assess where our risk is and make sure that we are covered for those eventualities'.

'We have a PR contingency plan, too, in case something awful goes wrong – for example, if a child goes missing. We have listed the documents we will need to provide to the press so we can react quickly and efficiently'.

What I'd Do Differently

· · ·

Assess Risks Earlier

'I would have looked at what could possibly go wrong sooner. When we first had a member of staff leave it floored us for a while because we didn't have a response'.

Source: Wendy Shand

SUMMARY

In this chapter, we concentrated on the core fundamental aspects of risk assessment and evaluation using industry benchmark, illustration and case examples and activities.

CHAPTER 11

Risk Management and Mitigation

INTRODUCTION

So far we have seen how risks can be identified, categorised and assessed. We are now going to look at the ways in which risk can be managed and mitigated.

Of course there are other facts that help any successful project to completion and many of these have been covered earlier in the workbook. These include effective project planning system and policies, employing skilled project managers and other staff, management and leadership skills, sound and effective reporting and information systems and financial control.

Here, we are talking about the management of identified risks.

There are several broad approaches and we will consider each of them.

GENERIC RISK MANAGEMENT STRATEGIES

Avoid the risk
Cancel the project
Build in fail-safe systems
Overspecify
Test, pilot and trail
Risk mitigation or reduction
Take precautions to prevent or moderate the risk
Accept the risk
Share the risk
Limit the risk over time
Transfer the risk
Insurance
Swaps
Hedging

AVOID THE RISK

Perhaps, this can be done in situations where a different choice between options results in a safer strategy, but one with fewer rewards.

CANCEL THE PROJECT

The ultimate way of avoiding risk is not to carry out the project at all. Many projects go ahead because of the mistaken belief that it will never happen. What can go wrong will go wrong, and the courage to take a decision to cancel a project when there is pressure on all members of staff to deliver is very strong. A corporate culture that embeds the acceptance of risk avoidance based on evidence would clearly prevent this. However, there are few rewards available for not doing something.

Effective use of risk assessment tools and the quantification of risk set against the possible returns are the best way of managing this process.

FAIL-SAFE AND RISK AVOIDANCE SYSTEMS

The second way of avoiding risk is to build fail-safe systems so that identified risks simply cannot occur. Lock (2008) gives the example of a Japanese car manufacturer who built in a fail-safe system that meant that unless all required components were in place, the machinery designed to fit those components would not work.

OVERSPECIFY

Overspecification at key stages of the project can help avoid risk being experienced. The Forth Bridge is a good example of an overspecified project; designed after the disaster on the Tay Bridge, the engineering specification was significantly more than required.

TEST, PILOT AND RESEARCH

The role of testing and piloting in marketing projects is well known. Testing in direct marketing involves the small-scale sampling of alternatives in order to optimise the outcome of any activity. The use of computer-simulated test marketing of new product launches is now used prior to the actual launch of new products to try to avoid the expense of actually launching the products, an expensive process even on a regional basis.

MITIGATION OF RISK

Take precautions to prevent or moderate the risk. There are many actions we can take to reduce the impact of risk. These have been covered to some extent earlier in the section but they include some or all of the following, depending on the nature of the risk and its potential impact.

- Training
- Employment strategies
- Leadership and risk culture
- Backup and security of data
- Excellence management reporting systems
- External inspection and consultancy
- Financial auditing and fraud prevention

ACCEPT THE RISK

The fact that certain risks can be accepted is obvious. The key aspect is that the risks are identified, categorised and assessed for impact and those that cannot be accepted are actively managed.

SHARE THE RISK

Risk can be spread and managed through the use of multiple partners in a project.

LIMIT THE RISK OVER TIME

Risk can be limited by completing tasks stage by stage and reassessing risk after the completion of each intermediate stage. It is therefore possible to limit the downside risks after the completion of each stage and to cancel the project should the assessment of the impact of risks outweigh the advantages from the completion of the task.

MANAGING RISK THROUGH INSURANCE

The transfer or spread of risk is something that is very much in the news. The use of insurance to transfer and control the impact of risk, however, has been around since Edward Lloyd started his coffee house in the City of London in 1688. Here, traders and merchants came together to exchange information to manage the risk involved in importing and exporting goods by sea.

There are four main types of insurance:

1. Insurance relating to legal obligations or liabilities
2. Insurance against loss or damage
3. Insurance relating to personnel performance and activities
4. Insurance against financial loss

In many cases, insurance can be a legal obligation. These relate to laws and regulations as well as to conditions that are laid down in commercial contracts. It may be that a company that is employing a sales promotion agency will want to build in insurance against overredemption, for example.

Other liability insurance may cover failure to meet expected professional standards, resulting in negligence claims, environmental damage and loss relating to property, compensation for bodily harm due to accidents and professional liabilities.

CASE EXAMPLE – Indemnity Insurance

About CIM Insurance

We are very happy to launch our CIM Insurance scheme, set up specifically for members of the Chartered Institute of Marketing. After discussions with CIM, we have managed to secure rates we feel are extremely competitive and this is the reason we have the Institute's backing. Using our unique online system, cover can be purchased from start to finish within minutes – no hassle with paperwork!

We have taken our time to launch this scheme, ensuring that the premiums charged and the cover given are right for your needs. This has now been achieved, and using our unique online facility, consultants can now purchase cover, from start to finish, within five minutes.

The scheme was put together with the members in mind and uses single source underwriting for each specific section. That is to say we do not obtain quotes on each individual enquiry, but have in place prearranged premiums and cover with one insurer. We then continue to monitor the competitiveness of our underwriter during the year and any adjustments, or change of underwriter, will occur at the end of our scheme policy period.

However, the underwriters we do use have been with us for a number of years, therefore ensuring premium stability.

The scheme is available in two formats, both of which provide the widest cover available for the most competitive premiums.

1. Business Activity
2. Marketing Consultant

Limit of Indemnity

Choice of Limits from £100,000 up to £2,000,000 for any one claim and in the aggregate during the Period of Insurance.

Territorial Limits

Worldwide, excluding United States/Canada, their Dominions or Protectorates or as varied or excluded in the Schedule.

Interest

1. Negligent/Breach of Duty
2. Negligent Misstatements
3. Intellectual Property Rights
4. Defamation
5. Loss of Documents
6. Dishonesty of Employees

Source: Trafalgar Insurance, 2009

All parties involved in the project should be adequately covered for any liability.

Insurance that is required by legislation includes those relating to health and safety at work.

With much of this, professional advice should be sought from internal legal counsel or external lawyers and insurance advisors.

Professional bodies may also be able to offer advice and access to preferential rates.

LATENT DEFECTS RISK INSURANCE

This insurance will cover damage relating to problems in design or materials.

ACCIDENT AND SICKNESS INSURANCE

This will cover sickness or injury relating to key staff.

KEY PERSON INSURANCE

This covers loss relating to illness, injury or death of named personnel.

PECUNIARY INSURANCE

This covers financial loss relating to a variety of causes, for example, late completion of projects. Export credit insurance is an example of this.

CASE EXAMPLE – Export Credit Agency

ECGD, the Export Credits Guarantee Department, is the United Kingdom's official Export Credit Agency. Our aim is to help UK exporters of capital equipment and project-related goods and services win business and complete overseas contracts with confidence.

We provide:

a. Insurance to UK exporters against non-payment by their overseas buyers;

b. Guarantees for bank loans to facilitate the provision of finance to buyers of goods and services from UK companies;

c. Political risk insurance to UK investors in overseas markets.

We work closely with exporters, project sponsors, banks and buyers to put together the right package for each contract. With almost 90 years of experience in new and developing markets across the world, our knowledge can help you in unfamiliar environments.

Source: ECGD, 2009

EXPORT CREDIT INSURANCE (ECI) – THE FACILITIES

Buyer Credit Facility

Under a Buyer Credit Facility, a bank makes a loan to an overseas borrower in order to finance the purchase of goods or services from an exporter carrying on business in the United Kingdom. In order to enable the bank to make that loan, ECGD gives a guarantee to the bank in respect of the borrower's repayment obligations. The exporter is then able to claim disbursements from the loan as and when amounts fall due for payment under the terms of its export contract with the overseas buyer.

Supplier Credit Financing (SCF) Facility

Where a buyer requires credit terms of at least two years for an export contract, an SCF Facility allows the exporter to pass the payment risk to its bank in respect of the credit portion. It also allows the exporter to receive cash from the bank upon shipment of the goods or for work done under the contract. ECGD's support is in the form of a guarantee to the bank, under which ECGD guarantees payment to the bank of the finance it has made available, if the buyer defaults on the credit.

Lines of Credit

An ECGD-supported Line of Credit can provide UK exporters of capital goods with a quick way to access finance made available by a UK bank to an overseas borrower. Such facilities can be set up to enable (i) a variety of overseas buyers to purchase unrelated capital goods or services or (ii) an individual buyer to purchase a wide range of capital goods or services for a particular project. The loan funds are used to pay exporters once the goods are exported or services are performed. If the borrower fails to repay any part of the loan, ECGD's guarantee to the UK bank means that it still receives payment in full.

Project Financing Facility

Where a UK exporter is involved in a major project overseas, ECGD may give its support to project financing arrangements under which the banks providing finance rely primarily upon the revenues of the project for repayment. Like a Buyer Credit Facility, ECGD's support takes the form of a guarantee to the lending banks in respect of a loan, which they have made to the project company. Amounts are disbursed to the UK exporter from this loan as and when amounts fall due for payment under its contract with the project company.

RECOURSE

When ECGD provides a Buyer Credit or SCF Facility to a bank, which has financed an export contract, ECGD may wish to have recourse to the exporter (and possibly its parent company where appropriate) for all or part of any claims payment which it has made to a financing bank, at a time when the exporter has failed to meet any of the conditions of its contract except when that failure is neither material nor substantial or has been caused by certain specified circumstances outside of the exporter's control.

INSURANCE FACILITIES FOR EXPORTERS

Export Insurance Policy (EXIP)

The Export Insurance Policy protects an exporter against not receiving payments to which it is contractually entitled under a capital goods contract as a result of the occurrence of specified commercial or political risks.

Bond Insurance Policy (BIP)

A Bond Risk Policy provides protection in the event of a bond being called unfairly and for calls made as a result of specified political events, and is provided in respect of an export contract where a Buyer Credit Facility, an SCF Facility or an EXIP is being provided for that contract.

Overseas Investment Insurance

Investment Insurance provides cover in respect of political risks (including expropriation and restrictions on remittance) in respect of certain investments made in developing countries.

(*Source*: ECGD, 2009)

Uninsurable Risk

- There are risks that will not be insured
- Those where the chances of the risk occurring are too high
- Where there is no possibility of spreading the cost of insurance across organisations insuring similar risks
- Where there is no actuarial data from past events to quantify the risk
- Where there is the potential of gain from the insurance

Where to Acquire Insurance

Insurance can be obtained from a broker or directly through an underwriter. The cost of insurance can be high and certain risks, for example those relating to terrorism, may be more expensive or hard to insure.

Other Ways of Transferring Risk

Use Swaps, floors ceilings collars and other hedging instruments.

We often read in companies' financial statements that they made exceptional gains owing to exchange rate differences or a loss was made owing to increases in commodity prices. These profits and losses are created out of circumstances that lie beyond the organisations' core business and most companies try to minimise their downside impact through a variety of control mechanisms.

Depending on the sophistication and size of the business, other companies will try to maximise the upside benefits. Companies like Mars and Hershey, for example, will have a significant impact on the value of the price of cocoa in international markets.

SUMMARY

Here, we were able to concentrate our thinking and exposure to ways of protecting our organisations and ourselves by mitigating risk via:

a. insurance
b. finance and
c. transfer

CHAPTER 12

Controlling Risk

INTRODUCTION

Like in all management disciplines, control mechanisms need to be introduced from the outset of the process and permeate throughout to allow review and contingency. Risk management is no different.

RISK REPORTING AND DOCUMENTATION

The process of recording the outcome of projects and the risks attached to them is a key aspect of risk management systems. As Chapman and Ward (2003) state in their excellent book on risk management, documentation provides six core benefits.

1. Clearer thinking: writing clarifies thinking.

2. Clearer communications: documentation including risk reports and audits provides a valuable means for communication between remote parties to a project.

3. Familiarisation: documentation helps new project team members to come up to speed with project issues.

4. A record of decisions: documentation should explain the rationale behind key decisions.

5. A knowledge base: the knowledge gained from one project can help the efficient implementation of subsequent projects.

6. A framework for further data acquisitions: analysis helps organisations understand better the information requirements for project management.

There is also an obligation for effective risk reporting for Public Limited Companies (PLCs).

The Financial Reporting Council (FRC) publishes guidelines to directors about risk reporting and these are outlined below.

CASE EXAMPLE – FRC

Assessing the effectiveness of the company's risk and control processes

Some questions that the board may wish to consider and discuss with management when regularly reviewing reports on internal control and when carrying out its annual assessment are set out below.

The questions are not intended to be exhaustive and will need to be tailored to the particular circumstances of the company.

Risk assessment

Does the company have clear objectives and have they been communicated so as to provide effective direction to employees on risk assessment and control issues? For example, do objectives and related plans include measurable performance targets and indicators?

Are the significant internal and external operational, financial, compliance and other risks identified and assessed on an ongoing basis? These are likely to include the principal risks identified in the Operating and Financial Review.

Is there a clear understanding by management and others within the company of what risks are acceptable to the board?

Control environment and control activities

Does the board have clear strategies for dealing with the significant risks that have been identified? Is there a policy on how to manage these risks?

Do the company's culture, code of conduct, human resource policies and performance reward systems support the business objectives and risk management and internal control system?

Does the senior management demonstrate, through its actions as well as it policies, the necessary commitment to competence, integrity and fostering a climate of trust within the company?

Are authority, responsibility and accountability defined clearly such that decisions are made and actions taken by the appropriate people? Are the decisions and actions of different parts of the company appropriately coordinated?

Does the company communicate to its employees what is expected of them and the scope of their freedom to act? This may apply to areas such as customer relations; service levels for both internal and outsourced activities; health, safety and environmental protection; security of tangible and intangible assets; business continuity issues; expenditure matters; accounting and financial and other reporting.

Do people in the company (and in its providers of outsourced services) have the knowledge, skills and tools to support the achievement of the company's objectives and to effectively manage risks to their achievement?

How are processes and controls adjusted to reflect new or changing risks, or operational deficiencies?

Information and communication

Do management and the board receive timely, relevant and reliable reports on progress against business objectives and the related risks that provide them with the information, from inside and outside the company, needed for decision-making and management review purposes? This could include performance reports and indicators of change, together with qualitative information such as on customer satisfaction, employee attitudes etc.

Are information needs and related information systems reassessed as objectives and related risks change or as reporting deficiencies are identified?

Are periodic reporting procedures, including half-yearly and annual reporting, effective in communicating a balanced and understandable account of the company's position and prospects?

Are there established channels of communication for individuals to report suspected breaches of law or regulations or other improprieties?

Source: Financial Reporting Council, 2005

RISK MONITORING

Once the project is underway, there are a range of tools that are employed to monitor and to report on the risks identified.

A risk log is maintained and regularly updated by the project team.

New risks that might emerge through the project are also logged and assessed using the range of tools outlined above.

If an identified risk occurs, then this is also is recorded along with the outcomes.

If an identified risk does not occur, then this too is recorded, as the avoidance of identified risk is clearly a vital part of the risk management plan.

The management of the risk log is an active process and forms a key element of the risk management documentation.

The FRC also publishes guidelines on monitoring risk, which are given below.

MONITORING

Are there ongoing processes embedded within the company's overall business operations, and addressed by senior management, which monitor the effective application of the policies, processes and activities related to internal control and risk management? (Such processes may include control self-assessment, confirmation by personnel of compliance with policies and codes of conduct, internal audit reviews or other management reviews.)

Do these processes monitor the company's ability to re-evaluate risks and adjust controls effectively in response to changes in its objectives, its business and its external environment?

Are there effective follow-up procedures to ensure that appropriate change or action occurs in response to changes in risk and control assessments?

Is there appropriate communication to the board (or board committees) on the effectiveness of the ongoing monitoring processes on risk and control matters? This should include reporting any significant failings or weaknesses on a timely basis.

Are there specific arrangements for management monitoring and reporting to the board on risk and control matters of particular importance? These could include, for example, actual or suspected fraud and other illegal or irregular acts, or matters that could adversely affect the company's reputation or financial position.

(*Source*: Financial Reporting Council, 2005)

RISK REVIEW

The review process can be broken down into four distinct phases:

1. Immediate reactions, success and failure should be quickly assessed and analysed
2. Immediate action to counter negative outcomes
3. Long-term review and evaluation
4. Systems and strategy review and evaluation

The reasons for review are many, and most are common sense. A risk review within the project enables us to:

a. Assess personal or team performance
b. Prevent future risks being experienced
c. Identifying training needs to help avoid future risks
d. To identify issues with processes and systems

Risk review can be done by:

Members of the project team
By staff independent of the project
By external audit teams

Finally, risk-aware companies might choose to work towards BS 31100. This is a key standard for risk management and gives a clear view on how to develop and sustain effective risk management.

BS 31100 is a key standard for risk management. It gives an understanding on how to develop, implement and maintain effective risk management within your business.

Using BS 31100 effectively can help increase a company's effectiveness.

■ (Information about the standard can be obtained from the British Standards Institute at http://www.bsigroup.com/en/Standards-and-Publications/Industry-Sectors/Risk/Project-risk-management/)

CONTINGENCY PLANNING

The final document is the contingency plan. Should risks occur, then such a contingency or crisis management plan will be implemented. The plan should identify:

1. Alternative actions relating to key risk events occurring
2. Resource allocation to implement remedial activity
3. An alternative project timeline

CASE EXAMPLE – FDS

Crisis Planning at FDS – Crisis management and business continuity planning

Here's what I learned about contingency planning after a disaster

When arsonists destroyed the head office of Kent-based field marketing agency FDS Group, chairwoman Alison Williams ensured that her 75 employees were rehoused and the business fully operational within three working days. Here is what Alison did – and what she learned.

What I learned

People are your biggest asset

'Having a disaster-recovery plan which helped to relocate the entire business within days sent out a strong, positive signal to our customers. But we still learned a great deal-especially about the people we work with'.

'Our contingency-planning routines meant that our data was backed up off site, so we knew the data was safe. We made use of our contacts in the local business community and had two temporary offices to view within 24 hours. We couldn't make any moves without our insurance company's approval, so our company secretary was tasked with making sure that a loss adjuster was on site by noon the day after the fire. When he arrived, we thrust a licence for potential premises under his nose and got his approval to move in there. He was surprised at this-but realised we had a business to run and co-operated on this point'.

'I've never been so proud of my staff-and suppliers fell out of the woodwork to help us too. Postmen came round to help us clean up and rescue items after they had come off duty, delivery drivers kept our parcels safe and Compaq, our IT supplier, worked alongside our own IT department from Monday night to Wednesday night non-stop, bar a few snatched naps on the floor'.

Engage an insurance assessor

'We found dealing with insurance companies both stressful and time-consuming as they were not always helpful or co-operative. Once we had an insurance assessor on our side who knew the ins and outs, we were much more comfortable. Our assessor was paid a percentage of what we received from the insurance. But he more than covered his costs in terms of reducing our stress levels and negotiating a better settlement with the insurers than we could have done'.

Clients need to be reassured

'There was no time to dwell on the situation-most of our clients are blue-chip businesses that demand and deserve continued service no matter what, and our offices were totally uninhabitable'.

'Getting operational as quickly as possible was the best way to reassure our clients. Having got a fully functioning office, we spent a lot of time making sure that our customers' confidence in us remained strong. Members of our management team held several informal meetings with customers to share ideas and resolve any residual problems. This demonstration of our commitment showed that we were very much back in business and valued our customer's needs above everything else'.

What I'd do differently

Devote more resources to winning new business

'I would have ensured I allocated more staff working on winning new business in the period after the fire. Our main priority was to keep the business we had, so new business development went on the back burner for a few months. As a result, our profits growth dipped from 35 per cent a year to just 8 per cent in the year following the fire'.

Check insurance levels are adequate

'Generally we were well covered, but only had one year loss-of-earnings cover. In hindsight, this wasn't enough and it took a lot of work to prove our losses in one year. We've now got three years-if we had that cover at the time, it would have taken a lot of the pressure off'.

Source: Business Link, 2009

Contingency plans should be regularly rehearsed; this may reveal issues with the plan and allow corrections to be made before they are tested in reality. All partners involved in the business should also be involved in testing.

Testing may be paper-based using a workshop environment or may involve quasi-live testing using communications cascading to test the efficiency of communications between those involved in implementing the contingency at all levels. Finally, a full-dress rehearsal can be used; this is expensive but may be useful.

London First publishes an excellent guide to continuity planning, which can be accessed at

www.thebci.org/London%20Firsts.pdf.

SUMMARY

In this section, we have seen the value of risk planning within the overall project plan. It could be argued that in today's difficult business conditions, assessment and mitigation of risk is a core business function.

We looked at the risk management plan and saw that the plan involves:

1. Risk audit
2. Risk evaluation
3. Risk report
4. Risk treatment
5. Risk monitoring and reporting

We looked at the range of techniques that marketers could use within this framework to boost the upside opportunities that exist within a project and to counter and manage the downside risks.

Senior Examiner's Comments – Section Three

This section of the syllabus recognises the contemporary and practical alignment of risk management in an applied organisational context and the associated interface with fundamental marketing management. Although alluded to at Level 4, the extent of exposure to these concepts has been limited thus far. Consequently, it was necessary to introduce a relative depth within this unit while at the same time endeavouring to balance the knowledge and application requirements at Level 6. To that end, and with particular reference to the current business environments, it is necessary to explore, appreciate and understand that operating within organisational and environmental dynamics, risk exists.

This is not a new concept. As marketing students, the necessity to audit dynamics is fundamental to the marketing management discipline and from the outset, at all levels, we are introduced to the aspects and elements of risk. At Level 6, a framework for the actual and potential manifestation of these risks is explored.

There is no guarantee for success and a realisation of this dictates the imperative of a rigorous, disciplined and formal control regime.

Therefore, there is a need to incorporate the concept of risk within an organisation's orientation. This is not about negating innovation or implementation but more about assurance in practice.

The students will be expected to assess situational risks, for example, relating to communications projects, Customer Relationship Management, New Product Development to name but a few, within the parameters of marketing projects and therefore should examine these relative to the undertakings in Section 2. So, in essence, the concepts and frameworks that candidates already know and understand from a core marketing perspective should now be applied in relation to risk.

To that end, students will drill down and concentrate their skills in auditing, planning and control.

The additional elements here are in effect around contingency and impact. As a result, a relative examination of mitigation and a critical analysis of recommended actions are sufficient.

We do not want to reinvent the wheel here. This section purely brings to the fore elements of marketing that have been implicit and inherent from the discipline's inception and through its evolution. Common sense is the order of the day, and given the current business environment, the management of or more importantly the control of risk is even more imperative. We want the student and the practitioner to embrace an enhanced mindset. It is no longer enough to be customer focused and market orientated. In addition, it is necessary for our analysis and decision making to fully incorporate a pillar that identifies analyses and plans to control and limit risk.

Therefore, risk is no different to any other aspect of the marketing discipline. In essence, concentrate on identifying the problems and implementing the solutions. Again, these will be specific and in context. An assessment brief will be published, which will highlight the core areas of identification, analysis, mitigation and control.

Relative to the different briefs at each assessment diet, a core element of the risk management process will always be highlighted in context. These will be published at the beginning of each examination board. To reiterate, we are not trying to reinvent the wheel, and industry standards and benchmarks alongside professional models should be used when analysing, evaluating, managing or controlling risk.

Within this element of the assessment, the expectation is on the application of approach to manipulating identified and previously analysed and evaluated risk. This will have already happened within the previous two sections and consequently only summarised. Here, we give the opportunity to elaborate and present these findings in a predirected format that extracts data, information and manipulation for the award of marks.

Where, however, innovative and original approaches to monitoring and measuring risk are presented, these will be rewarded.

- A core appreciation of risk assessment and management concepts, principles and techniques is expected here.

Bibliography for Section 3

Buttrick, R. (2005) *The Project Workout*, 3rd edition. Prentice Hall, Harlow.

Charrel, P.-J. and Galarreta, D. (2007) *Project Management and Risk Management in Complex Projects*. Springer Dordecht, The Netherlands.

Chapman, C.B. and Ward, S.C. (2003) *Project risk management: Process, techniques and insights*, Second edition. John Wiley and Sons, Chichester.

CIM 2005 Marketing and the 7 Ps.

Financial Reporting Council (2005) Internal Control, Revised Guidance for Directors.

Gardiner, P.D. (2005) *Project Management*. Palgrave Macmillan.

Housden, M. and Thomas, B. (2002) *Direct Marketing in Practice*. Butterworth Heinemann, Oxford.

Lam, J. (2003) *Enterprise Risk Management*. Wiley Hoboken, New Jersey.

Lewis, J.P. (2007) *Mastering Project Management*, 2nd edition. McGraw Hill, New York.

Lock, D. (2003) *Project Management*, 8th edition. Gower, Aldershot.

London First (2003) Expecting the unexpected: Business continuity in an uncertain world.

Lynch, G.S. (2008) *At Your Own Risk*. Wiley Hoboken, New Jersey.

Maylor, H. (2003) *Project Management*, 3rd edition. Prentice Hall, Harlow.

Reuvid, J. (2008) *Managing Business Risk*, 5th edition. Kogan Page, London.

Ringland, G. (2006) *Scenario Planning*, 2nd edition. John Wiley & Sons, Chichester.

The Faculty of Finance and Management of The Institute of Chartered Accountants in England & Wales, *Risk management for SMEs*, October 2002.

Turner, J.R. (2007) *Gower Handbook of Project Management*, 4nd edition. Gower, Aldershot.

WEB SOURCES

http://www.pwc.com/extweb/home.nsf/docid/5169CCB510A5F16F85257383004E3E8E (accessed February 2009).

Brand republic 2009 www.brandrepublic.com/News/210917/lot-learn-Hoover-free-flights-fiasco/ (accessed January 2009)

http://step.nasa.gov/doc/ap233_concept_model_12th_draft_dwo_3.ppt Risk diagram is on slide 47 (accessed March 30, 2009).

http://www.trafalgar.uk.com/asp/CIM-professional-indemnity.
asp?a=0&useDef=1&sp=cim&r=0.

http://www.businesslink.gov.uk/bdotg/action/detail?type=ASE%20STUDIES&itemI
d=1075070373 (accessed February 2009).

http://www.businesslink.gov.uk/bdotg/action/detail?type=CASE%20STUDIES&item
Id=1081872608 (accessed February 2009).

Reuben, A. (2009) HBOS risk control 'dumbed down' BBC News http://news.bbc.
co.uk/1/hi/business/7892079.stm (accessed March 30th, 2009).

http://www.bsi-global.com/en/Standards-and-Publications/Industry-Sectors/Risk/
(accessed February 2009).

http://www.bsigroup.com/en/Shop/Publication-Detail/?pid=000000000030191339
(accessed February 2009).

http://www.marketingpower.com/Community/ARC/Pages/Additional/Definition/
default.aspx (accessed March 30, 2009).

Project Management for Analysis, Planning, Implementation and Control (Weighting 40%)

4.1 Critically evaluate different approaches to developing a culture of project planning within the marketing function and the organisation

4.2 Critically evaluate soft and hard projects in the context of marketing and consider the differences in terms of project implementation

4.3 Develop the main stages of a marketing project plan, identifying the activities, estimating time and cost, sequencing of activities, and assess the competency and skills required of the people needed to deliver the project

4.4 Critically assess the importance of and techniques for establishing the marketing project's scope, definition and goals relative to the organisational marketing plan

4.5 Utilise a range of tools and techniques to support project planning, scheduling, resourcing and controlling of activities within the project to enable effective and efficient implementation

4.6 Utilise a variety of methods, measurements and control techniques to enable effective monitoring and measuring of progress throughout the project to ensure that it is completed to specification, on time and within budget

4.7 Critically assess the main techniques for evaluating effectiveness, success or failure of a marketing project on its completion

119

CHAPTER 13

Foundations of Project Management

INTRODUCTION

Historically, project management (a specific form of management) was given limited attention in academic texts in marketing. However, professional project management has gained recognition, and this is now recognised as a factor impacting on marketing performance. Its importance in effective marketing and business success is reflected in the focus in CIM marketing qualifications.

KEY DEFINITIONS

Project	A temporary endeavour undertaken to create a unique product or service (Project Management Institute, 1996).
Project management	Project management is managing non-repetitive activities to ensure that they achieve time, cost and performance objectives.
Project life cycle	Project life cycle addresses the time from the initiation of a project (with the start of its planning), through its implementation and then on to termination, when the project ceases to exist.

Managing projects has always been a central part of marketing activity.

Project work in marketing includes planning events, marketing research and campaigns, for example. Further, marketers are commonly involved in strategic, cross-functional projects, such as new product or market development, or implementing change within the organisation. However, until recently, project management was a general part of marketing professionals' management activities.

Marketing gained professional status in the United Kingdom in the 1980s on the basis of the body of knowledge that underpins effective marketing. Project management developed over a similar period, and like marketing, it developed a body of knowledge of best practices and terminology. With the increasing pressure to ensure marketing effectiveness, it is clear that use of the insight from the project management discipline adds to marketing projects. Effective project implementation – regardless of topic – needs good project management.

This first chapter in Section 4 specifically centred on Project Management provides the foundation for the following chapters. As such, it is focused on understanding about projects and the factors that influence their success. Later chapters will build on this foundation and add more detail on terminology, tools and techniques.

FOUNDATIONS OF PROJECT MANAGEMENT

The Project Management Institute (PMI) (1996) defined a project as 'A temporary endeavour undertaken to create a unique product or service'.

On the basis of this definition, projects:

- are transitory or for a determined period of time (i.e. they are not routine or continuous activities);
- will achieve a specific, unique output;
- have defined start and end dates (i.e. they are not open-ended business activities).

At the simplest level, there are three core stages of a project, which are referred to as the project life cycle. Most sources expand these basic three, but they are always there, underpinning more complex models.

1. *Beginning* (or initiation) – A project begins – or is initiated – once its planning starts.

2. *Implementation* – A project takes place during the implementation stage. This is simplistic. To many people, including the consumers or users, this is a time of more high visibility, but a very significant part of the time can be spent in the planning and design processes.

3. *Termination* – Once the management process is complete (including the 'shake down' and project review), the project no longer exists and is terminated.

Often, a project's output, such as a new product or a new branch layout, will exist at the end of the life cycle, but this is no longer a project and no longer a project management responsibility. For example, a project to develop a new product would be managed as a project, but the launched product is a marketing management responsibility.

So, project management focuses on managing *non-routine* activities and situations effectively. The unique aspect of projects brings complexity or uncertainty in their management, as the situation is different and needs to be managed in a way that addresses the novelty and complexity.

Projects involve different participants, processes and resources from its beginning to its termination in order to meet its outcomes.

Further, different organisations with similar marketing projects, similar budgets, timescales or performance would result in different project approaches, staff involved etc. The organisations' goals, culture and resources would impact on the nature of the project.

These different elements of projects add to its uncertainty.

1. *Input uncertainty* – the skills and labour that is available, and the desired mix of skills; the roles, experience, reliability, involvement, availability and solvency of suppliers and subcontractors and material provision.

2. *Process uncertainty* – the risk involved in the project activities, including the work breakdown, the integration and linking of activities, management of bottlenecks and understanding critical paths; the speed of environmental changes; stakeholders' expectations and interrelationships and even project politics.

3. *Output uncertainty* – the fit of the results with client and stakeholder requirements, specification changes and market changes during the project.

CASE EXAMPLE – MasterCard

MasterCard and sports sponsorship

The aim of MasterCard's sponsorship of these globally watched events is to enable themselves and their worldwide partner institutions to develop their existing and new businesses.

MasterCard has sponsored prestigious football events since 1990, when it was the Official Card and Official Product Licensee of Italia 1990. It continued in this World Cup role until the 2006 FIFA World Cup. It is also the Official Payment System of the various PGA (Professional Golf Association) tours and events.

However, VISA card claimed the sponsorship rights for 2010 and 2014 World Cups from FIFA.

Source: www.mastercardintl.com/www.corporate.visa.com/av/about_visa/sponsorships/fifa.jsp

ORGANISATIONAL CONTEXT FOR PROJECTS

'Every strategic initiative in a firm involves change management—and that is best accomplished through the tools, tactics and techniques of project management…

Project management thus becomes the enabler, the vehicle through which all strategic change happens. The project itself is the gap filler, the bridge between what is and what will be' (Baker, 2008).

Projects should be undertaken within the usual corporate and functional (e.g. marketing) planning processes. The objectives set at different levels will set the foundations of strategy. Project management is often critical in ensuring that required changes are put in place.

Projects can be set at corporate level, departmental level, product level and market level or even across departments or geographies. Top-level projects include culture change throughout the organisation, new market entry or even implementation of an enterprise system. Departmental, product and market levels could include research or promotional projects for marketers, or the roll out of a new sales force reporting system as examples. Projects that span departments and geographies include new product development projects.

It is clear that projects are an essential part of the business activities at all levels. The challenge then is to prioritise and manage these appropriately to meet the organisation's needs.

Organisations and departments typically have many projects at any given time. Projects need to be aligned with the organisation's strategic priorities, and prioritised to ensure that the organisation's resources are focused on the priorities of the organisation. However, Rad and Levin (2008) comment that often projects appear like 'floating' islands and are not best integrated into the organisation.

They recommend the use of Project Portfolio Management (PPM), which enables organisations to select, resource and implement projects to ensure that the right projects are selected on the basis of their benefit to the organisation, and also taking account of the organisation's resources. Most PPM approaches result in a prioritised list of the most important projects. The project at the top of the list should have priority over others, and resourcing decisions should follow.

This PPM approach is not limited to new projects, but places a check on the relevance of projects as the organisation's strategy changes. As the portfolio term implies, this assessment must not only apply in the original selection decision, but also review the project at key stages to test the current alignment with the organisation's objectives and strategy, failing which can result in early project termination.

While the discipline of a PPM approach is perfectly logical, it must be recognised that the outcomes are often not. If a number of projects are competing for approval at a project board or equivalent, then the relative strength of support and positions of power of the project champions will often influence the decision.

External conditions may have an impact – it is much harder to get approval for expenditure during recessionary times, so otherwise important work will be cancelled or postponed.

It is often more difficult to make a case for large-scale in-house projects that do not *directly* relate to profitability. For example, a company may have a series of databases within separate departments that are not integrated. To rationalise them into a consolidated database with much more potential for improving, Customer Relationship Management could give significant longer-term returns. The problem is that it might be forgotten when a campaign shows good results that it was the refined database that pointed the way to better targeting of new clients.

ACTIVITY 13.2

Make a list of projects in your organisation and marketing department.

Consider whether these are strategic or operational projects, whether they are cross-department or within-a-department activities. Look also at the topics they address (promotions, products, culture, logos etc.).

- Who is involved in managing, supporting and working on these?
- What differences can you see between marketing projects and the routine work in marketing?
- Are these projects viewed discretely – i.e. managed individually – or managed as part of a portfolio approach?
- What are the implications of your findings?

Projects involve estimates of how long and costly the separate elements will be. Estimates can be optimistic or pessimistic. It is hoped that the staff involved in any estimating will try and be as rational as possible, but some subjective opinion is needed. This can colour people's attitudes in deciding on the viability of the respective projects.

CASE EXAMPLE – GlaxoSmithKline

GSK is one of the world's largest pharmaceutical companies. Project management is very important in its business success. A recent project has been to establish a global training programme to ensure that project management in Glaxo is at world-class level, with a common commitment to and understanding of company policies, attitudes to risk and discipline for managing projects.

Top management sponsored and championed the training programme, and project 'champions' were also identified within the strategic business units. These 'champions' helped build enthusiasm for the programme, and ensured that training materials were relevant to their SBUs. These approaches helped to reinforce the value of the programme to the company, and in using the materials.

In doing this, the project management training has resulted in relevance throughout the company, which enables cross-functional collaboration across the many GSK businesses.

Source: Alexander, J. (2008) GlaxoSmithKine: Improving global project management capability, *Chief Learning Office*, June 2008, 58–59.

ACTIVITY 13.3

What are the advantages of an organisation-wide approach to project management?
What problems could exist?
Does your organisation have a shared approach to project management?
Who, if anyone, champions a project management approach?

WHY IS PROJECT MANAGEMENT IMPORTANT?

Professional project management started on major projects, such as new airport developments or major industrial developments. In such instances, project managers were required to coordinate and control the development process and the interaction of all players (e.g. owners, funding agencies, developers, designers, contractors, suppliers, operators, regulatory bodies etc.). The complex nature of these projects meant that a formal management was required.

Successful project management in this sphere led to an awareness that organisations with strong project management were more effective than those that did not manage projects well. Project management then developed its 'body of knowledge' that has since spread to all sizes of projects across different functions and throughout organisations.

What is effective project management? Meredith and Mantell (2000) state that success or failure of a project is based on whether they have achieved targets on:

- Required performance (quality)
- Cost (money invested)
- Due date (delivery)

Traditionally, the key measure of success in marketing projects is achieving the *outcome*. A successful project is thus completed within the allocated time and cost and to the desired quality or results (such as achieving a level of awareness or encouraging people to trial or specific sales results).

The three core issues – performance, cost and delivery – are clearly sound commercial issues. A delay in the launch of a movie may mean that it misses a period when demand is traditionally high. A delay in launching the movie in one market may result in pirated copies there. A poor-quality soundtrack or editing of a movie may limit customers' enjoyment and reduce the possibility of word-of-mouth referrals. Failing in one of these areas results in loss of revenue and customer satisfaction. Exceeding the budget will also impact on profitability.

A further criterion is increasingly being added as a requirement for marketing projects – customer satisfaction. In this instance, customer satisfaction may refer to the internal customer – the person who commissions the project – or the organisation's customers.

However, customer satisfaction may be more complex to assess. Consider the following domestic examples.

Family A requires new fitted wardrobes. The joiners say it can be done to time and cost. When these are fitted – on schedule and to the agreed cost – they find that these are not substantial enough to withstand standard family use, and were broken within days.

Family B had the same budget and delivery, but were advised part-way through the contract that the original doors were potentially not going to survive 'normal' family use. They were advised that that they should exceed the budget given the requirements, which resulted in a delay in getting the replacement doors. However, once they were installed, they were glad they had added to the cost, and the late delivery was seen as acceptable.

Where outputs are clear and fixed – such as delivery dates, cost or quality – it is easy to set requirements. However, sometimes other factors may turn out to be more important. This is a problem in marketing projects, where uncertainty and change may require changes in the project definition (or *scoping*). However, this still must be managed well.

ACTIVITY 13.4

Find out about past projects in your organisation. Ideally, you should be able to identify some that are deemed to be successful and others that were unsuccessful.

What criteria are used to define success and failure of these projects?

Many organisations undertake research to calculate the costs of late delivery, or poor performance or monitor the cost/profit levels.

Identify whether this research exists in your organisation. What does this tell you about the importance of these outcomes?

PROJECT MANAGEMENT AND MARKETING PROJECTS

Project management's contribution is now widely recognised as important within the functional areas of organisations. Marketing initiatives, activities and campaigns often fit the above definition of projects. Professional project management gives attention to the various players, tasks and outcomes for their success.

The consideration of project management will first address the types of marketing projects (activities), how these are undertaken (people and processes) and why they do it (strategic goals, competitive position and customer satisfaction). Success results from their effective coordination and integration.

CASE EXAMPLE – Amgen

The biotechnology company Amgen uses large-scale 'meetings' (conferences) as part of its marketing activities. These meetings could be for staff, customers, distributors, regulators etc.

Formerly, these could be arranged by any member of staff, but since 2001, meetings of more than 10 people must be made through a specialist meetings department, which is part of Amgen's Sales and Marketing function.

The department has contracted organisations to manage many of the routine aspects of meetings – one company manages registrations for the meetings, another manages sourcing and monitors the meeting process and budgets. By outsourcing routine tasks to other companies, the Amgen staff members can focus on managing the more strategic aspects of project management.

Amgen found that small meetings (generally fewer than 75 bedrooms, less than four days and for Amgen staff only) were taking about the same amount of internal staff time as larger and more high profile projects. Amgen decided to make these smaller meetings the so-called turnkey process, with all the work being outsourced to a meetings organiser once the venue had been chosen.

Some Amgen meetings project managers have been promoted to other project management roles within the company.

Source: Kovaleski, D. (2006) The relationship matrix, *Corporate Meetings & Incentives*, July, 25(7), 14–19.

TYPES OF PROJECTS

The differences between projects indicate how they should be managed. Brown (2000) sees projects as spreading across a continuum, with complexity increasing on a number of dimensions.

These dimensions include:

- Budget size
- Time span
- Human resources involved
- Complexity of tasks
- Cross-functional involvement
- Coordination required

Simple projects, characterised as low budget, short term, simple tasks, within a functional domain, would require more administrative management. Those that are more complex, with higher budgets, often with people from different departments (and maybe organisations) and spanning a longer term would require more sophisticated project management.

ACTIVITY 13.5

Refer to the list you developed in Activity 13.2.

Use these, and any other factors that you deem appropriate, to distinguish between the projects in your organisation. Which types of projects are you most involved with currently? What does this suggest about your role in managing projects?

Obeng (1994) takes a related approach to characterise four distinct project environments, with differences in process uncertainty (i.e. what to do) and the level of outcome uncertainty (i.e. what can be achieved) and named the four resulting categories.

1. *Paint by numbers* – Projects are low in process and outcome uncertainty, e.g. installing point of sale (POS) displays in retailers' outlets. The outcome is the same – the installation of the POS display – and the process (the way in which it is implemented) would be similar. However, differences, such as environmental factors (e.g. existing store design), time issues (e.g. minimising staff and customer inconvenience) and cost issues (e.g. adaptations for a given situation) mean this is not a completely routine process. Often, organisations have process protocols or manuals detailing core processes. These types of projects are considered 'hard' projects, because of their fixed processes and clarity of outcome.

2. *Making a movie* – Projects are low in process uncertainty and high in outcome uncertainty. Producers and directors know what is involved in making the movie, although the topic, location and people vary. However, predicting the success of the movie is difficult. Projects such as new product or advertising campaign launches often have a similar pattern of high costs and a high risk of failure. These projects need clear, precise definition of outcomes, and stakeholders' expectations must be managed throughout the process. Timescales and budgets must be tightly controlled.

3. *The quest* – Projects are high in process uncertainty and low in outcome uncertainty. These projects have focused outcomes, but it is not clear how or when this will be achieved. Some exploratory development projects, such as AIDS cures for pharmaceutical companies, are in this category. Progress and resources reviews throughout these projects are essential to keep within cost. Further, focus is essential to keep the project on target.

4. *The foggy project* – Projects are vague in what is involved and in the expected results, so they have no set process and uncertainty outcomes. The original dot-com companies, like boo.com and lastminute.com, were foggy projects in their development stages, with little to guide them. Foggy projects need control over costs and level of risk. Marketers need extensive research to minimise the outcome failure, but time and cost management are important for these projects. Project managers need to manage stakeholder relationships as the project develops.

ACTIVITY 13.6

Refer to your earlier list of projects from your organisation.
Review how the organisation manages each of these types of projects.
Which of Obeng's categories are most difficult to manage?

ACTIVITY 13.7

Review Obeng's four project categories and the Pepsi case.
Is this project of strategic importance for the company? What are the implications of your view?
Would the range of activities involved in the above project be classified as one project or several projects? Why?

CASE EXAMPLE – Pepsi

In 2008, Pepsi unveiled its new logo – its second change in a decade. The process took five months, and it is believed to have cost more than $1 million for the brand experts who came up with the new logo, with its 'series of smiles', with a Pepsi smile, a Diet Pepsi grin and a Pepsi Max laugh.

Modern consumers are not impressed with global megabrands, and Pepsi saw a more engaging brand logo as a step towards a more relevant brand. The brief was to make the logo 'more dynamic', fun and alive, and so better suited to the more individual culture of consumers, and the growing range of soft drinks.

However, changing the new packs is only one part of the new logo launch. Think about how many billboards, vending machines, retail displays and other promotional items need to be replaced throughout the world. And then there are vehicles, packaging, uniforms etc. Coordinating the replacement of all old logos would cost hundreds of millions of dollars. For this reason, the full launch will not take place until 2009.

Source: Zmuda, N. (2008) *Advertising Age*, 10/27/2008, 79(40) 6.

SUMMARY

This chapter has given the background to project management. The following chapters will then detail the processes and issues involved in managing projects. By this stage, you should be thinking about which type of projects could be potentially suitable for your assessed work.

CHAPTER 14

Project Process

INTRODUCTION

This is the second chapter addressing Section 4 of the syllabus, on analysis, planning, implementation and control of projects managed by the marketing function, or in which the marketing function is a participant. This chapter details the key issues undertaken in the three main stages on the project management life cycle, through from initiation and implementation to termination.

This chapter forms the foundation for later chapters, which detail key project management issues, processes, tools and techniques. Notably, these include Chapter 15 that deals with project management culture and organisation; Chapter 16 that deals with project management outcomes and Chapter 19 that deals with project management methodologies. Cross-referencing to the other chapters is extensive within this chapter. While each chapter is able to stand alone, these chapters ultimately form an integrated and detailed framework for project management. (This is similar to studying the marketing mix, where elements are addressed separately, but need integration in practice.)

KEY DEFINITIONS

Initial project plan	An initial project plan is an outline plan, detailing the outcome and key participants and stages. This is developed in the initiation stage of the project.
Integrative project plan	The integrative project plan is the detailed project plan, developed and used throughout the implementation stage. This includes details of schedules, budgets and resourcing.

PROJECT PLANNING ISSUES

This chapter focuses on the key management concerns in the three generic project management stages (project initiation, implementation and termination), which were introduced earlier. It expands on key issues in each stage, where these are not addressed in later chapters.

THE PROJECT BEGINS – PROJECT INITIATION

The first phase of a project is the initiation phase. Commonly, several aspects are considered at this time. The key elements are:

- Project selection
- The project manager role
- The project organisation
- Initial project planning

PROJECT SELECTION

Project selection involves the evaluation of different potential projects, and then deciding which and how many to support. Project management literature distinguishes between two broad approaches to selecting the 'right' project:

Subjective, e.g. market needs, or a competitive requirement
Objective, e.g. with detailed profitability calculations, and resource requirements

This project selection process implies that there are several potential projects under review at one time, which actually may not be the case in every instance.

The following are common ways of initiating marketing projects:

A casual comment from a senior manager identifies a need or opportunity, which then initiates a project. In project management terms, these are often called 'Sacred Cows' – unlikely to be killed off, even if they are not a real priority.

A member of staff has an idea or a commercial need, and makes a case for a project to a senior manager, and this initiates the project.

A gap in the market or in performance (such as a loss in market share or the possibility of failing to meet the marketing objectives) initiates awareness of a problem and triggers the search to find causes and potential solutions. These potential projects may be urgent and discrete.

These are not 'best practice' as defined in theory. Ultimately, organisations and departments have to make decisions about where best to allocate limited funds.

ACTIVITY 14.1

Does your organisation have any 'sacred cow' projects?
   If so, how much attention is given to them?

Project selection involves both objective (quantitative) and subjective (qualitative) criteria. For example, an organisation may decide to go ahead on a project for the launch of a new product because of:

- a 'window of opportunity' that exists
- past experience
- the potential profit and
- the degree of risk

One manager or a small team of people may make selection decisions. This could be discussed and debated, with varying levels of supporting information.

Applying this approach to marketing, selecting projects may therefore involve consideration of several projects, such as the adoption of a new CRM system, new product development projects and market research initiatives, alongside each other.

The pressures of ROMI mean that project ideas should face some evaluation. However, often it is difficult to gather information for marketing project ideas at this early stage. Many are exploratory projects, where it is difficult to be able to predict the financial or competitive benefits at the time of commissioning (see Section 2 on making a business case).

As mentioned in Chapter 13, the criteria for selecting different projects should be developed to choose between projects. These criteria should be related to the organisation's objectives, strategies, resources and constraints. Possible topics for evaluation of different projects include:

1. *Production factors*, such as ease of manufacturing, availability of materials, supplier reliability

2. *Marketing factors*, such as the potential market size, the extent of competition, seasonality, likely product life cycle length, brand extension prospects

3. *Financial factors*, such as investment required, funding availability, profit margins, time to break even

4. *Personnel factors*, such as staff requirements, skills required, training required, impact on staffing etc.

5. *Administration and miscellaneous factors*, such as spread of project team, infrastructure requirements, government regulations

Once the key factors are identified, projects can be evaluated against criteria using rating schemes. Ideally, these criteria should be:

- Objective, rather than subjective
- Prioritised or weighted

Clearly, supporting data is required to enable the best projects to be identified.

The first rating approach identifies different criteria, reflecting their importance to the success of the project, and then evaluates potential projects against these criteria. There is no fixed number of criteria. Some organisations make judgements on 3–6 criteria, while others have more extensive listings.

In Table 14.1, each criterion is scored on a 0–5 point scale, where 0 signifies 'not applicable', 1 is 'poor' and 5 is 'excellent'. This implies that the higher the score, the better the project prospects. This information should then guide the company in its choice of project.

Table 14.1 Project scoring

Project A	Project B	Project C
Marketing		
Potential market size		
Strength against competition		
Brand extension prospects		
Financial		
Profit margins		
Funding sources		
Speed of reaching break-even		
Production		
Availability of materials		
Compatibility with existing equipment		
Ease of manufacturing		
Project overall score		

Be careful with the choice of dimensions here and their wording, as this can change the emphasis. For example, high cash requirements would be a negative factor, rather than a positive one.

A more advanced version of this could add weightings to show the relative importance of these criteria. This is similar to the types of rating and weighting approaches in the directional policy matrix.

These rating processes must be used with care. Some managers believe them to be overly simplistic. Unless used with sound supporting data, they may merely quantify subjective views. Further, the criteria selected may not be good predictors of success of a project. Criteria that are universally applicable for ease of comparison may be inappropriate for some novel projects.

Despite their limitations, these tools seek to reduce the subjective influences by focusing on how projects meet key criteria and to focus managers on justification of projects.

The outcome of this choice process is the initiation of the project, which is the project start date.

ACTIVITY 14.2

In your organisation, are projects considered as they emerge, or in a formal project evaluation process?
    What are the advantages and disadvantages of your organisation's approach?
    If you have a formal evaluation process, what criteria are used to evaluate these projects?
    What method of selection is used?

ACTIVITY 14.3

In your opinion, would this project have faced competition against other projects? Why?
    Is the appointment of consultants the start of this project?

PROJECT MANAGER

A project manager should be appointed once the project is chosen. The nature of this role will depend on the project size and project organisation. For example, the project manager for a major programme like Pepsi's global brand and packaging changes (Case Example in Chapter 13) will be very different from the project manager role for the launch of a small business's website. Some roles will be full-time posts, and others will be part time. Some project managers will be senior managers providing leadership and control, whereas others will take a more administrative role.

Cross-functional teams for large projects will increasingly have a project manager with formal project management qualifications. Marketing projects are often managed by marketing managers or other members of the marketing team. In some cases, a senior marketing manager may be considered as the project leader, but day-to-day project management is performed by a more junior staff member.

Chapter 13 identified the trend to professional project management. This is increasingly linked to professional qualifications in project management. Some companies have career development programmes in project managers, and these are not exclusive to full-time project managers.

Currently, unique project management roles in marketing departments are comparatively rare, although these are increasing. They are common in agencies though, although they may have different job titles.

CASE EXAMPLE – IBM

IBM is one of the world's top brands. Much of IBM's work involves planning and implementing complex bids and solutions. These are essentially project management tasks. IBM has implemented project management training for many staff involved in these roles.

Subsequently, IBM sought to measure the benefits of project management training, and their research showed that projects with qualified project managers were less likely to fail. Alongside this, these results also showed increased customer satisfaction. These trained project managers also received more positive project approvals. In a pattern similar to Heskett's service profit chain, these project managers were also less likely to leave IBM (suggesting higher job satisfaction). Staff retention is important – other companies seek PM-qualified staff.

Source: Wheatley, M., 2005

THE PROJECT ORGANISATION

Defining the project organisation is a key part of the initial project planning. The structure and composition of the project team organisation needs to be defined at this stage in the project, as the initial project plan requires input on different aspects of the project. The project organisation is related to the scale of the task and the potential budget available.

Organisation-wide projects tend to have cross-functional teams, spanning different functional specialisms. The team in marketing projects is often drawn mainly from the marketing department, and may also include marketing services organisations, often in addition to other work responsibilities. Financial or IT staff are also often involved. Project teams can be ad hoc groups, which work in the project as part of their normal activities, or a specialist focused project team.

ACTIVITY 14.4

Think about the people who should be involved in your assessed project. Do not just think about who is 'usually' involved in these projects – think about the types of roles that need to be part of the project team.

Students need to start thinking about the roles and involvement of each of these in the assessed project. You will need to consider this more formally later in your work.

THE INITIAL PROJECT PLAN

The final stage in the project initiation process is the development of an initial project plan. This document is not a full working plan but should detail:

- The project scope and objectives
- The proposed start and finish dates
- The deliverables (i.e. the desired outcomes or results) should also be specified
- The project management methodologies to be used
- Any constraints or limiting factors, such as time, money, people or equipment, weather conditions, cultural problems
- Any potential risks in the project and detail how these are going to be managed and monitored
- The overall budget for the project

Outline plans detailing the required tasks, likely budgets and schedules, are prepared by the key participants, scrutinised by the project manager and the project team and integrated into a 'composite' project plan. Trade-offs between time and resource issues may be required to integrate these different plans. This integrative approach is essential for project buy-in from team members and uses their expertise.

The project manager normally is responsible for coordinating the composite plan and gaining its approval. Marketing projects tend to be less detailed than some other technical disciplines at this point because of the types of project tasks (as defined in Chapter 13). Most detailed planning takes place in the project implementation stage in marketing.

Bidding to host the Olympics requires outline project planning to gain the approval of the Olympics committee. London 2012 prepared a written document as part of their submission to the Olympics Bid Committee.

Amongst the issues, the London 2012 organisation have to consider are media operations, transport, security, venues etc., and the work to bring these to the required standard. These issues were considered individually and in detail in their bid document – an initial project plan – and plans for key areas at: http://www.london2012.com/plans/index.php

ACTIVITY 14.5

Look at the key areas in the outline project plan listed above.
Explain how these link to the determination of success and failure in a project.

PROJECT IMPLEMENTATION

The majority of the work in projects takes place within the project process. However, this section is shorter than that for initiation. This is because many of these issues are considered in the following chapters.

The first part of implementation is developing outline plan into an integrative project plan (Meredith and Mantell, 2000), including:

1. *Overview of the objectives and scope.*

2. *Detailed objectives* – profit, technical and competitive aspects of the project.

3. *The general approach of the managerial and technical aspects of the project* – how this links or deviates from existing approaches and projects. This would include the choice of the appropriate project management methodologies.

4. *Contractual requirements* – the reporting processes of all parties, the review processes, agreements with third parties and schedules. Information on changes to the plan, including rescheduling, the substitution of suppliers or cancellation of the contract should also be determined.

5. *Schedules for the work* – the components parts and key milestones in the progress of the project. The project scope should be broken

down ('decomposed') into parts. This depends on the chosen work breakdown structure (WBS). At its simplest, a WBS is a structured and itemised 'to do' list. Each task should be detailed, with time estimates. Timings should be agreed by the project manager.

6. *Resource issues* – the detailed budget should be included, as should the project budget monitoring process.

7. *Personnel requirements* – the skills required, and processes and criteria for selection of employees, training programmes.

8. *Methods and standards of evaluation* – mechanisms for collecting and storing data on the progress of the project should be determined.

9. *Potential problems or assumptions* – including terrorist threats, weather problems or governmental bureaucratic factors that might be outside the project manager's control.

10. *Contingency planning* – most plans have some form of contingency planning. The approach and allowances for this is part of the main project plan.

A summary checklist is presented below.
Does the project plan detail:

- What the project and the project management will achieve? (objectives, outcomes and scope)
- How will the project be managed? (methodology)
- When will the project be complete? (timings)
- Who will do what tasks? (roles and responsibilities)
- When will each task be done? (work breakdown system)
- What resources are required? (resources)
- How much money is required and available? (budget)
- What risks exist and how will these be managed? (risks)
- How will the project be evaluated? (evaluation)
- What contingency planning is in place? (contingencies)

Identifying these components disguises the complexity of project planning and implementation. It is often said that the negotiation begins after the project scope is agreed. From then on, project management is about the 'soft' factors of managing people, reconciling the project's interests with those of other participants.

The 'hard' aspects of project management are budgeting and scheduling. Scheduling develops the sequence of tasks, both independent and interrelated, that will be undertaken. These are presented in a series of subschedules and charts can be prepared from the master plan, detailing what will happen when, by whom, and detailing the interfaces and the milestones for the tasks. Detailed scheduling turns the project plan into action plans, based on the WBS (Work Breakdown Structure).

Revised schedules are prepared as issues emerge. Rescheduling does not always mean delays in completion, as contingencies – for time or budget – may be built into the project plan. If the delays exceed this, and there is no flexibility with the delivery date or resources, ceasing the project should be considered.

Project management methodologies guide the stages works schedules, and software simplifies the preparation and presentation of plans and revised plans. These can be presented by task, person, stage or date, and in the preferred format. Schedules are commonly presented pictorially as Gantt charts, as these are easy to understand.

ACTIVITY 14.6

The main responsibility for preparing these promotional materials was with the agency.

What Volvo involvement would be required in the project organising team?

Would local markets see local plans only or the whole campaign plan?

CASE EXAMPLE – Volvo Cars

Volvo Cars' Dalarö campaign.

Volvo Cars' launch of the S40 was an excellent example of project management in marketing.

This multimedia campaign by Volvo, created by advertising agency MVBMS Fuel Europe, ran in the United Kingdom, Ireland, Spain, Belgium, Netherlands, France, Luxembourg and Switzerland. The theme, the 'Mystery of Dalarö', was presented as a mini-documentary (or 'mockumentary') reporting on a Swedish town of Dalarö, a small coastal village 40 miles from Stockholm, where 32 families in Dalarö bought an S40 Volvo on one day.

The campaign was launched in the United Kingdom on 26 January, 2004 and continued until 31 March, 2004.

Similar schedules operated in European markets, using blends of radio, television and cinema advertising, which linked to online sites with the full-length Dalarö film. Online banner advertising drove traffic to the site. TV advertising ended on 14 March, but websites remained available throughout the campaign. Detailed schedules were prepared to manage and communicate consumer promotions and to share these with dealers, so they could plan local activities to support and build on the national multimedia campaigns.

Volvo used this campaign to create a 'buzz' through its unusual approach. Timescales needed to be consistent across the participating markets to ensure that the spoof nature of the film was not disclosed early in the campaign.

PROJECT TERMINATION AND PROJECT EVALUATION

The third stage of the project management life cycle is project termination. A decision to terminate a project occurs when one or more of the following occur:

a) A project is superseded, possibly by competitors' actions or a new technical development.

b) A project is 'killed' by management before completion, often once its internal sponsor leaves or another initiative has greater priority or fit.

c) Projects are deprived of funds and starve to death.

d) Projects are integrated into the routine activities of an organisation.

The decision to terminate a project is not the end of the project management process, which ends after the project evaluation. Evaluation determines how well the project met its objectives, including time, cost and quality, and how well the needs of its stakeholders were met. Project evaluation helps develop learning to guide future projects.

Small projects may have informal reviews, but larger projects need formal reviews. Although evaluation takes place throughout the project, an integrated evaluation at the end of the project reflects on reasons for success and failure that may be missed in operational management. Project audits are rigorous reviews, using a structured approach, and often undertaken by an independent party.

SUMMARY

These generic stages and the content of plans at each stage should be helping you firm up your thinking about your assessed project. Many of the issues are addressed in more detail in the following chapters. However, you should now have a clear idea about the things you are required to undertake.

CHAPTER 15

Project Orientation

INTRODUCTION

This chapter looks at project management orientation, culture and project team structures and interaction. Marketing orientation is firmly based on a shared organisational culture that is committed to customers. Likewise, project-oriented organisation and culture is viewed as a factor in project success. This chapter will begin with looking at the organisational orientation to projects. It will later move to project-oriented cultures and team culture.

KEY DEFINITIONS

Project-oriented organisation	A project-oriented organisation defines 'Management by Projects' as an organisational strategy, applies temporary organisations for the performance of complex processes, manages a project portfolio of different project types, has specific permanent organisations to provide integrative functions, applies a 'New Management Paradigm', has an explicit project management culture and perceives itself as project oriented (Gareis)
Project-oriented culture	A project management culture is characterised by empowerment of employees, process orientation and continuous organisational change to support project work.
Project culture	The culture of specific project teams, i.e. the culture associated with a specific project.

PROJECT-ORIENTED ORGANISATIONS

A project-oriented organisation (POO) is characterised by the following basic elements:

Sees 'Management by Projects' as a central element of organisational strategy.

Has a portfolio approach to managing projects.

Has a project management culture and organisation, with use of project teams to solve business problems.

Has central co-coordinating and facilitating structures to support projects, but changing project structures for project duration.

Project-oriented organisations tend to be 'flatter' than traditional organisations, with less functional organisation (i.e. less focus on e.g. finance, marketing, HR, type departments), as illustrated in Figures 15.1 and 15.2. Further, they are more 'fluid', with project teams forming and disbanding with the dynamics of the marketplace and business requirements. These characteristics have been labelled as a 'new management paradigm'.

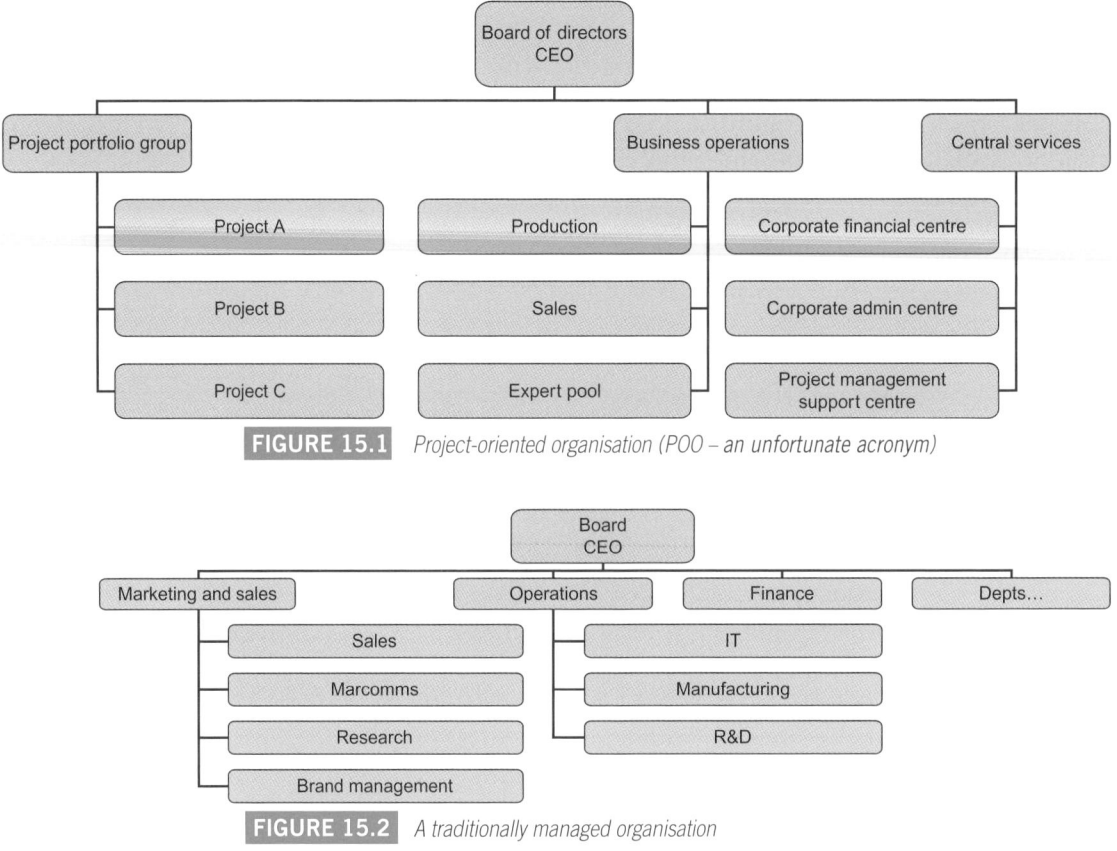

FIGURE 15.1 *Project-oriented organisation (POO – an unfortunate acronym)*

FIGURE 15.2 *A traditionally managed organisation*

ACTIVITY 15.1

Identify examples of project-oriented organisations in marketing.

ACTIVITY 15.2

Is your organisation traditionally organised, or does it have a project-oriented organisation? What are the implications of this on business success?

The type of organisational orientation to projects and the size, topic and uncertainty of the task also impact on the nature of the project team. The main project team organisations include:

- *Project structures* – Project teams are formed around specific projects. This is suited to large, long-term projects, and is common in high-tech companies, management consultancies or advertising agencies. Typically, project teams are put together at the start of the project and disbanded at the end of the project. Project teams encourage commitment from the team members. The teams can be built quickly, so are ideal when speed is critical. However, new jobs may not be available for project team members on completion of the project.

- *Functional organisations* – Projects are managed by a department or function of the organisation, which has the responsibility for allocating staff to the project as required. People commonly work on several projects, and knowledge and experiences are shared within the department as the projects develop. This does not remove people from future career opportunities in their department. It is best suited to more administrative tasks, where cross-functional input is not required. Often, this 'multitask' activity does not give sufficient support to priority projects, unless management actively manages time according to the priority of the project portfolio.

CASE EXAMPLE – Nokia

Nokia opened a design studio in London in 2007, with more than 125 different designers, with a range of design specialisms. However, in 2008, Nokia sought to add about 20 freelancers to this team, to work on branding, experiential, print and interaction design, for an international marketing campaign for three weeks.

Nokia finds that freelancers work well with its in-house teams. The designers will come up with Nokia's 'flagship'

campaign in what is known as a charrette – an extensive period of activity on design work.

The marketing campaign is being led by Lowe Worldwide, which is also managing the recruitment for Nokia.

Source: Pacey, E. (2008) Nokia assembles design team for global marketing campaign. *Design Week*, 23(39), 3.

■ *Matrix organisations* – A team operates between the two extremes of pure project and functional organisations. Matrix organisations are often closer to one of the previous two forms of project organisations. For example, some matrix teams have a project team that is not separated from the parent department, but have people with part-time responsibilities to the project. This is called a strong matrix organisation, and is closer to the project organisation. A lone committed project manager, with access to resources from other departments, is a weak matrix organisation. Matrix structures often result in multiple demands on departments and key personnel. The project manager's control can be reduced because of these multiple demands. Often, the most critical projects may not get the attention required.

CASE EXAMPLE – Mars

Mars offer Galaxy and Dove brands in various international markets. The former brand name was used in the United Kingdom and the Middle East; the latter was used in China. While the brands looked alike, each market had ownership of its strategy.

In 2003, Mars decided to change Galaxy's strapline of 'Why have cotton when you can have silk'? It was decided to develop a global strategy for the brand.

A global project team was established, with people from Mars, and members of their research, communications and design agencies. Starting by understanding the global market, the outcomes were to redesign and implement the global brand strategy.

Mars decided to keep the existing brand names, but with a common global positioning. The packaging and the shape of the chocolate bar was changed to give a more sensual look (and feel for the chocolate bar shape), after the company realized that its customers saw this as indulgent, and the product experience starts with anticipation before eating the product.

The results from this project showed the success of the new strategy. Brand value has increased by 42% since 2004, at just under $1 billion in 2007. Some individual markets grew substantially – sales in the United States more than doubled over this period.

Source: Anon (2008) *International Marketing*. 6 November, Supplement, p. 14.

ACTIVITY 15.3

Look at the Nokia and Mars' case studies.

These include a variety of types of participants.

Compare these approaches with your organisation's approaches to project organisations. What factors drive your organisation's approach to forming project teams?

PROJECT-ORIENTED CULTURE

The 'new management paradigm' refers not just to the project-oriented organisation, but also to the culture – or values and norms – of project orientation. Typically, a project-oriented culture (POC) has a management style that focuses on:

- Empowerment of employees
- Process orientation
- Continuous organisational change

ACTIVITY 15.4

Think about an organisation with a reputation for fast and successful innovation. How would you characterise the culture and structure of this organisation?

Now think about another organisation that has failed to innovate in response to changes in the market.

How would you characterise the corporate culture and structure of this organisation?

Ideally, a project organisation and culture should be led from the top of the organisation, and guided by an experienced project manager. However, sometimes top managers themselves need to be convinced of the change from functional management. It is commonly accepted that successful projects (using a project management approach) are a good way of showing the value of this approach.

As project-oriented cultures tend to be cross-functional and collaborative, existing organisational structures must be realigned round project teams. Associated with this, business processes need to be addressed, including:

Reporting lines need to be clarified – these may be cross-functional and could be contradictory.

Budgeting processes may need to be realigned round projects, so HR responsibilities, training, appraisals, etc. may move from functional management.

PROJECT CULTURE

The term project culture refers to the culture of specific project teams, that is the culture associated with a project. Like mini-organisations, these have values, norms and rules.

These in turn create:

- sociability (e.g. team unity and spirit) and
- solidarity (commitment to the goals and working approach)

This strong team unity and commitment further benefits the project cultures by clarifying the boundaries between routine work and a project, or between different projects.

CASE EXAMPLE – Land Rover

The advertising creative team format has been attributed to Bernbach at DDB agency, who brought people from the copywriting and art departments together. Since then, there have been many examples of successful partnerships of copywriters and art directors.

Agencies differ in how they use creative teams. Some form new teams for new projects, while others prefer long-standing partnerships. Creative teams do not always meet the clients, but can be briefed by an account director who acts as an intermediary.

An example of 'best practice briefing' involved Land Rover briefing a new agency, Craik Jones Watson Mitchell Voelkel. Land Rover wanted and needed a distinctive campaign, and to ensure that the agency delivered this, Land Rover hosted the account team (planning and creative people) at Land Rover's Warwickshire headquarters, where they were taken on a tour of the factory, and given the chance to experience driving the Land Rovers on the company's off-the-road driving track. The team was then shown an extensive stock of new Range Rovers, and given the brief: 'Sell those. As we have clearly failed to do. And don't suggest discounting our product – because we don't do that'.

The inspiration from the off-the-road driving, the understanding of the product quality and the company requirements led to a very successful campaign, based on the real understanding of why people buy cars.

Source: Partly based on: Kershaw, S. (2004) Creative masterclass on managing creative teams. *Direct Response*, 1 March.

ACTIVITY 15.5

Refer to the Land Rover case and answer the following questions:

Who are the members of the project management team for this campaign?

In this instance, what benefits resulted from Land Rover's approach to briefing the agency?

Project cultures differentiate the project and its team. Traditional aspects of differentiation, as used in marketing practice generally, are commonly used to build the culture. These include:

- A strong and distinct project name
- A project identity and logo
- Project songs, slogans, etc. (some of these may be more readily acceptable in different countries or cultures)
- Signs, symbols, decor and environment

CASE EXAMPLE – Coca-Cola

In December 2007, The Coca-Cola Corporation (TCCC) advertised for a Project Manager for Global Market Integration (GIM). This role was to lead the project and integrate the adoption of a GIM process for markets around the world.

The job involved managing the project process, the people and the operational activities.

Amongst the specific business process aspects of the project were to:

■ Identify timelines and deliverables for the local markets.

■ Prepare and manage the flow of documentation for translation for local markets, ensuring that local markets ensure correct translations, and on time.

■ Ensure that local markets understand and work to the processes of legal approval of work, working with approved Corporate Legal Counsel in local markets, and to the schedule.

■ Direct and focus IT resources to ensure quality.

FORMAL PROJECT MANAGEMENT AND MARKETING PROJECTS

While many organisations have simplistic project management approaches, job advertisements state that they are looking for 'good project managers' within the requirements for a range of marketing jobs. However, marketing projects differ on the basis of:

a) The type of organisation (project-oriented organisations or traditionally structured organisations)

b) The size and complexity of the project (e.g. strategic change vs. operational projects)

c) The scope of the project (e.g. cross-functional vs. one within a marketing department)

The larger, more complex or risky a project, the more important it is to have formal project management. Informal approaches to project management, especially in functionally organised organisations, are viewed as 'a sure path to disaster' (Brown, 2008). Accordingly, big projects increasingly use formal project management processes.

ACTIVITY 15.6

Refer to the project management in the Coca-Cola case study.

Review these tasks. How important do you think it is that this manager has a marketing qualification and background?

MARKETING-PROJECT INTERFACE – WORKING WITH INTERNAL TEAMS

Members of the marketing team often are involved in projects with other departments. These include R&D, purchasing, sales, HR, finance, IT. Historically, the 'silo' approach to functional organisations has meant that internal departments have different foci, performance criteria, interests and orientation. Moving into a cross-functional project team based more on a matrix structure can cause problems for them – especially as they are often expected to continue contributing to their normal workload.

Indeed, a leading consultant states that 'Not only is there a tension between the functional objectives, in many instances they are in fact 180 degrees opposite', (in Strategy and business, 2004). Further, as people in different backgrounds have different education and training, there is not even a common understanding of key terms.

A common example of where this conflict occurs is in project teams for CRM implementation. Cooper et al (2008) found that project team members are not used to the constant changes in the external business environment. Often, this threatens their 'comfort' levels, and they may not understand why the external changes were not evident earlier. Clearly, there is a need to avoid using jargon, to explain the reasons for requests (rather than assuming a common understanding of these) and to foster understanding generally.

ACTIVITY 15.7

Operational (or production) departments are often targeted to achieve cost savings, so sometimes 'cost-engineer' a product to a minimum level, with long production runs of products.

Marketers, trying to meet customer needs, may want to offer variety to different segments, with better quality.

You have been asked to attend a meeting to explain marketing's views to managers of the operational department.

Prepare a presentation to explain the marketing view to these operations people, taking account of their existing frame of reference.

SUMMARY

Here, we have examined the necessity to instil and encourage an approach to project management that should permeate throughout the organisation. The suggestion is that from a business philosophy standpoint, this could define and extend organisational orientation. Therefore, maybe a case exists for incorporating dual definitions within our business cultures?

CHAPTER 16

Project Scope

INTRODUCTION

This chapter addresses managing the project scope. Often, marketers have been accused of failing to manage project scope, and projects end up late and over budget. Managing project scope is identified as being critical in achieving company objectives and ROI (Return on Investment), achieving focused work, and gaining market and strategic benefits from projects. As with other areas, the recognition of its importance in effective marketing and business success is reflected in the focus in CIM marketing qualifications. The Standish Report (1994) identified that 84% of projects were not deemed to be successful. The major reasons for projects failing to succeed were:

- Poor or incomplete specification and requirements
- Changes in specification and requirements
- Unrealistic expected outcomes
- Unclear project objectives

KEY DEFINITIONS

Project scope	The work that must be done in order to deliver the project outcome, on time and cost.
Project scope management	'Project Scope Management includes the processes required to ensure that the project includes all the work required, and only the work required, to complete the project successfully. It is primarily concerned with defining and controlling what is or is not included in the project' (PMI (Project Management Institute), 2004).
Scope creep	Scope creep is where one or more aspects of the initial project scope is extended or expanded.

In 2004, the follow-up Standish Report 2004 reported that over 68% of large software projects are not completed, or do not fully meet their customers' needs. More than 80% of these problems are caused by 'runaway requirements'. Scope creep is the technical name for these 'runaway requirements'. Clearly, managing the project scope and reducing scope creep is a way of ensuring that the project is well focused, matched to customer needs and focused on the time and cost requirements.

Project Scope

The project scope refers to the work involved in achieving the outcome of the project, and all efforts and processes used in achieving the project outcome on time, and on cost.

This definition hides the fact that the most difficult element of managing project scope is in ensuring that unnecessary work is not undertaken. This is evident in the following PMBOK (Project Management Body of Knowledge, 2004) definition:

> *Project Scope Management includes the processes required to ensure that the project includes all the work required, and only the work required, to complete the project successfully. It is primarily concerned with defining and controlling what is or is not included in the project.*

The critical elements here are:

Defining what is to be included – what is within the scope of the project – and also identifying what is *not* required – what is outside the scope of the project.

Defining what is to be included needs attention to detail and the required information. Unless the project is fully thought through, then it is likely that there will be many actions and processes added to the project as it progresses. This often results in the project failing to meet its objects, budgets and outcomes.

ACTIVITY 16.1

Your CIM work is assessed. What are the consequences of you going outside the topic in your assessed work?
How much attention do you give to determining what is relevant and what is not relevant?

A starting point in identifying project scope is to determine the project stakeholders and their requirements.

Stakeholders are the people or organisations who are either part of the project process or affected by the project and its outcomes. These include:

- Senior management or other project sponsors
- Project participants, both within the organisation and external
- Customers and consumers

The term customer here can be confusing. You may have an *internal* customer for a project, such as a regional office, which wants a local market variant. However, the end customers and consumers may be retailers and consumers.

Often, marketing projects have more general terms of reference. For example, a project may be the development of a new product project team, whose role is to stimulate innovation or to develop a high-performing information system. It is hard to identify the scope, and define the work involved, with such general requirements.

Clearly, getting precise requirements out of the more general terms of reference is essential. These should be:

- Specific
- Measurable

These requirements tell us what we want or need. Next, we should consider how that can be done. As the full project plan is built and the business case and feasibility is reviewed, the remaining ART can be added to the SM above.

Precise requirements at this stage will save time and money at later stages, and increase the chances of a successful project.

An initial outline scope will usually be identified at the initiation stage of the project. This initial scope will be reviewed once the project begins, and this will be a major input into the scope definition.

You may need to spend time clarifying and reviewing the topic and acceptable outcomes in order to refine and define the project scope. Techniques like brainstorming should be used to identify different potential outcomes, and these should be presented to the sponsors (and sometimes to other stakeholders) for clarification.

Unfortunately, stakeholders commonly disagree over this. For example, a marketing manager and sales manager may have different requirements for the quality and timescale of a new product. Compromise is often going to ensure that the project does not meet any requirements.

The senior project sponsor (or champion) may have the ability to make – and impose – decisions on the requirements. However, totally ignoring other stakeholders could lead to them losing interest in the project. The project managers should try to negotiate a solution that ensures focus but retains commitment to the project from all key stakeholders.

Failing to address this fully at this stage will result in the project going out of scope at a later stage.

Table 16.1 Project requirements and priorities

Requirement/ outcome	Identified by	Priority level	Resulting specification

Table 16.2 Scoping matrix

Aspect	In scope	Out of scope
Geography	UK mainland	Northern Ireland, Eire, Scottish Islands, Channel Islands
Retailers	National supermarket chains	Symbol independents, e.g. Spar, Regional supermarket chains, e.g. Booths
Timescale	Within 12 months	Beyond 12 months
Focus	Existing project ranges	New products

Preparing forms that detail the requirements and priorities can help focus and involve key stakeholders and raise issues. A typical form is presented below in Table 16.1.

Remember though that project scope is about understanding what is outside scope, as well as in scope. Defining the parameters or boundaries may be essential in a project. You will often have to detail some activities or outcomes that are specifically outside the scope. These should also be expressly stated to avoid misunderstandings (Table 16.2).

Other elements that may be included in a scope statement are:

- Assumptions, e.g. about competitors or the state of the economy etc.
- Constraints, e.g. staffing level budgets etc.

ACTIVITY 16.2

Who are the stakeholders for your assessed project?
What are their interests and requirements?
How consistent are these?

CASE EXAMPLE – Scottish Enterprise

In 2005, Scottish Enterprise was involved in an innovative action project to improve marketing in SMEs.

Various subprojects were identified as part of this process, following discussions with stakeholders. Two scope statements from a presentation on this are presented below:

1. *Project Scope – Marketing Capability Research*
   Develop and define a framework/Model to enable the examination of the role of and function of marketing in innovative companies.

Compare with a comparable set of companies from UK and Europe.

2. *Project Scope – Marketing of Marketing – game based learning*

Design a series of related/inter-related games on the theme of marketing covering the key marketing disciplines to raise awareness of and increase understanding of marketing, its role and importance to innovative Scottish SMEs.

The game(s) is (are) to be used as an awareness-raising tool as opposed to detailed learning courses, introducing the concept of the marketing cycle, techniques and disciplines.

Source: http://www.wsep.co.uk/innovativeactions/downloads/papers/SGMinutes/SG6/SG%20Presentation%20of%20DG4%20Marketing%20Projects.pdf

ACTIVITY 16.3

Refer to the Scottish Enterprise case history.

Review these two scope statements. Identify activities and outcomes for each.

Identify two or three activities that are outside the scope of each of these projects, but which some people might have wanted to include.

Can you identify areas that could be further clarified?

The Project Scoping Document

Scope statements are short, but the project scoping process is more comprehensive in defining the project process. Scope definition is subdividing the major project deliverables into smaller, more manageable components, which are called the Work Breakdown System. Once this WBS detail is agreed, this scope definition should be put into a project scoping document.

The project scoping document details the project scope statement and the project approach. Like research briefs, project scoping documents vary in length, depending on the scale and outcomes sought. Some organisations have simple one-page templates, providing a summary document for all stakeholders. However, such brief projects may not provide sufficient information to manage the project scope.

Sponsors and managers should sign off the project scope document as 'agreed' to show that they are committing to this. This 'sign off' is called scope verification. It is also a form of deliverable. The project scoping document can then be communicated to all parties. Ideally, this project scoping document should then only be changed for major reasons.

The project scoping document can vary from business to business, but central elements are usually common to all even when the naming conventions are different. Possible headings could include some or all of the following, but do not be concerned if you see different names used elsewhere as long as the key elements are covered:

Project Name (and other project references)
Date and version of the scoping document

Background (can comprise the following)
Project scope overview
Project objectives
Project outcomes and deliverables
Participants, including departments and organisations
Key interfaces
Assumptions
Constraints
Risks
Budgets
Schedules (due dates)
Evaluation criteria
Project team readiness

Key Roles and Participants
Executive sponsor
Project manager
Project team and roles
Functional business experts (e.g. legal, financial etc.)
Technical experts (e.g. risk management, IT, brand management etc.)
Signature lines – sign off 'charter'

ACTIVITY 16.4

On the basis of the above materials, identify the problems that could exist if the project scope is not well defined.

Scope Creep and Scope Change

As the earlier materials identify, projects often change over time. Changes may be:

Mandatory – for example, resulting from changes in legislation.

Required – for example, where a change is necessary to solve a problem, such as an error in copy; or where something was not defined correctly in the first instance.

Optional – where an improvement to the original work is possible or desirable.

In many sectors, changes to a project plan may indicate that there has been a problem with the initial project goals or planning. However, as marketing is operating in a dynamic environment, often changes will be required by factors that are outside the control of the project team. For example:

- The target market segment is changing preferences, for example owing to the economic environment.
- A competitor has launched a new product.
- An external partner has withdrawn from the project.

Chapter 15 referred to research that showed that IT personnel were uncomfortable with changes caused by the changing business dynamics. These changes make managing scope in marketing projects difficult.

IT consultant Gopal Kapur (2004) says that project managers should act like guide dogs at times, and show 'intelligent disobedience'.

He comments that as the business environment and business knowledge change, then it is tempting for project sponsors to ask for changes in the project scope. However, he comments that some of these changes can be 'half-baked', and that accepting these can lead to extensive scope creep.

He advises project managers to learn to say no to their sponsors, using the analogy of a guide dog and its owner going to cross the road. If the owner wishes to cross the road, it is the guide dog's responsibility to sense the danger, and overrule its owner when appropriate.

Many people working on projects find managing unreasonable expectations from sponsors to be the most difficult. However, practicing 'intelligent disobedience' can result in a more focused project.

Scope creep is the term when work is added to the project after the scope has been established and agreed. Scope creep involves the changes to the project's ongoing requirements or activities increasing, without approved changes to cost and schedule allowances. Changes can and will occur, but these need to be managed through a scope management process.

Scope creep often changes many aspects, such as the timescales, costs and often outcomes. Scope creep often starts with small changes, in the total project or in one aspect of the project. These could include changes to fulfilment processes, or extent of catering menus etc. or venues. Often, these will have 'knock on' effects, such as cancellation charges, additional costs, delays in completion etc. Indeed, it is commonly believed that small incremental changes can lead to project failure. Although small, these can impact on the costs, schedule and the risk of the project.

Saunders et al. (2005) undertook research on the screening and evaluation criteria for new product development (NPD) research. They found that criteria for acceptance or rejection of product concepts vary through the NPD process. At the initial screening stage, there is a focus on the financial criteria. In the detailed screening and predevelopment stages, evaluation focuses on marketing issues, including the product, brand, promotional and market requirements. Post-launch, the decision makers are more interested in how the new product fits with the business commercially and with its production processes. Only financial criteria are highly valued at all stages of the project.

Avoiding Scope Creep

Scope creep can be limited by setting systems in place. Common approaches for avoiding scope creep include:

a) *Education of the project team or sponsor.* Explaining the impact of change on the project success often focuses people on avoiding the 'best' solution (e.g. adding every feature to a new product, rather than those specified in the project plan or that meet the target segment's requirements).

b) *Establishing processes for changes, such as a change request process.* Often, individuals make decisions that may impact on others in the project. Using formal processes for approving changes can stop regular and minor changes – or indeed more substantial ones. Change request processes can be initiated, with supporting documentation, which are to be submitted in writing to the project manager, and (depending on the scale of the change) reviewed by the project manager, the project team and/or the project sponsors. Clearly, agreed (and openly communicated) criteria to judge whether changes are appropriate (i.e. fitting to the project outcomes) and viable (in terms of value for money, ROI etc.) can reduce changes.

Projects should also have a project contingency fund to be used in case of essential changes.

ACTIVITY 16.5

A magazine referred to software vendor SAP as 'the company that holds patents on scope creep and late deliveries' (Hickens, 2008, p. 9).

What do you think the author meant by this?

Are the two areas scope creep and late delivery linked?

Agency Work

If you are in an agency or consultancy and working on documents, you should consider the following points to avoid 'scope creep'.

- Have a written agreement about what is involved in the project. Often, key points should be mutually agreed, not just discussed generally. Further, failing to detail the expectations and work involved can result in misunderstandings.

- Detail budgets in initial agreements, and specify what is and what is not included in these. Specify what receipts and evidence is required, and detail anything that requires separate approval or must be procured through your organisation's procurement processes.

- Detail the processes and steps to be undertaken, with estimated budgets and timescales. For example, if concept development is part of the process, identify the timescales and budgets associated with this. Often, clients do not understand expenditure on creative work, and may not understand background research costs in such stages.

- Detail reporting schedules and processes that are in place to manage focus and scope creep in advance.

- Detail the key contacts in between the organisations, as failing to do so may result in several parties getting involved. This can increase costs, cause misunderstanding and confusion between project members, and move the project off target.

SUMMARY

Managing project scope is the key to the success of a project. Project scope seems a rather straightforward concept. But it is commonly mismanaged, with people failing to take the appropriate actions and rushing to implement the project.

Initially, the scope of the project is planned. Then the scope will be defined, identifying the aspects that are in scope and out of scope, the project plan and activities, the deliverables and project acceptance criteria are defined.

Scope creep is a key problem that can derail projects. There are many reasons why project scope will change over time, especially for marketing projects. However, such changes need to be monitored carefully in case the project goes over-length or over-budget. Processes need to be set in place to monitor and control scope creep.

CHAPTER 17

Project Tools and Techniques

INTRODUCTION

Project tools and techniques are intended to give a structure and series of guidelines to work within. They are aimed at producing a logical and disciplined progression from the initial idea to the handover of the project (and sometimes a little beyond that when supplementary work is needed).

KEY DEFINITIONS

Work Breakdown Structure	This is 'A deliverable-oriented grouping of project elements that organises and defines the total work scope of the project. Each descending level represents an increasingly detailed definition of the project work'.
Deliverables	Tangible outputs from work undertaken, delivered to sponsors or managers that can be signed off.
Scheduling	Is the process of identifying and detailing the timings of project activities involved in completing the work.
Milestones	Mark the end point of an activity.

Several books report on marketing mistakes, many of which come from poorly planned marketing projects. Good planning is essential for project success, as is clear in the 6 Ps of project management: Prior Planning Prevents Poor Project Performance (this may be also be familiar in a rather more earthy form).

Often, the problems start with vague or poor project definition. Typically, projects have topics or requests such as:

a) Prepare a marketing communications plan for a new product launch or
b) Develop an improved new product development process

At one level, these seem fine. However, exploring these further highlights issues that must be addressed before planning can be undertaken.

- What sort of marketing communications plan?
- What targets – trade or consumer markets?
- What timescale?
- Are there any specific media to be used or avoided?
- What is meant by improved?
- How would this project be measured?

Initial scoping helps identify some aspects of the project, but this next stage of planning adds to the detail for the project plan and clarifies more precisely what is involved. There is an old saying that 'the devil is in the detail' and it is certainly true that you will have the devil of a time trying to successfully manage a marketing project if you fail to pay attention to detail.

The general process of project planning is the structure of this chapter.

1. Determining the work breakdown structure
2. Estimating timing and task duration
3. Determining resource requirements
4. Allocating responsibilities
5. Sequencing work
6. Developing the project schedule or network
7. Preparing the integrated planning document

The key project management tools will be identified within these headings. You should work through this chapter and consider how to incorporate the frameworks and tools in your assessed work.

DETERMINING THE WORK BREAKDOWN STRUCTURE

The key element of good project plans is the work breakdown structure. PMI defines the WBS as:

'A deliverable-oriented grouping of project elements that organises and defines the total work scope of the project. Each descending level represents an increasingly detailed definition of the project work' (Figure 17.1).

In his book *Project Management: Planning and Control Techniques*, Rory Burke argued a structure that is based on the four project phases of Concept, Design, Implement(ation) and Handover. He contends that each of these individual phases can also be broken down into the full four at a sub-project level. Let us take the Concept phase as an example. It would within it the original idea, but that idea would need to be checked and researched to put an overview together. That rough design overview needs to be built into enough of a case to allow the project to gain approval, and that is the

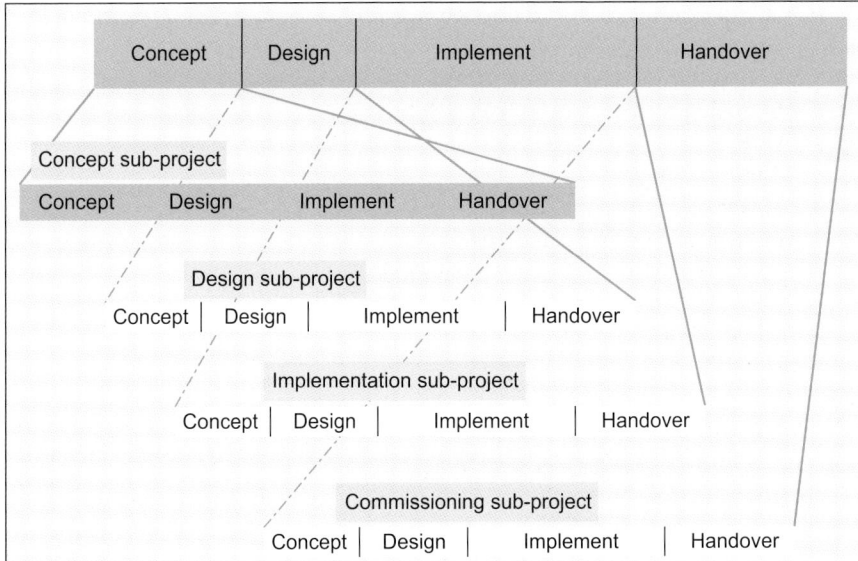

FIGURE 17.1
*Breaking down a project
into sub-projects
Source: Adapted from
Burke (2003)*

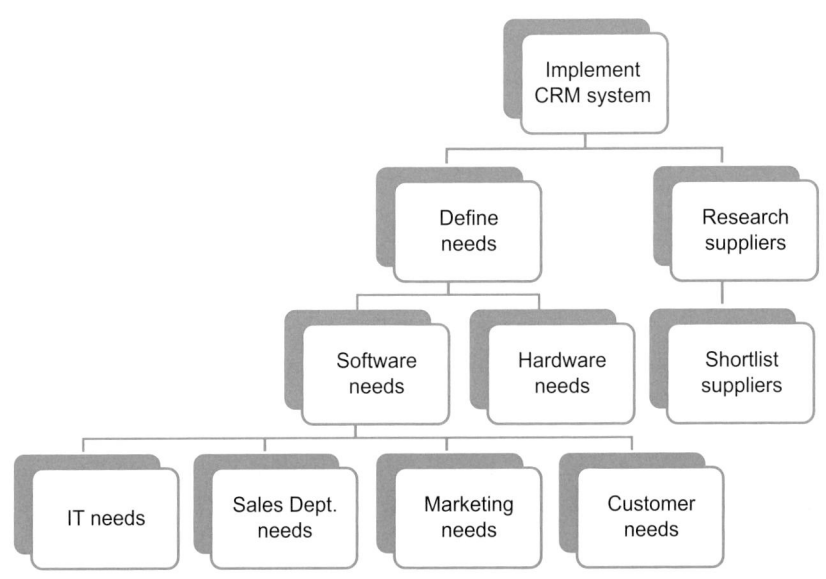

FIGURE 17.2
*WBS – implementing a
Customer Relationship
Management system
Source: Adapted from
Maylor (2005, p. 89)*

implementation that is aimed for. Once that has been gained, then there is a handover to those responsible for the next stage in the process.

The WBS is a structured hierarchy of the work that needs to be accomplished on a project. This organises work in an organisational chart-type structure, with different levels showing how goals, objectives, topics etc. can be broken down into increasingly detailed activities (see Figure 17.2).

1. Define the needs – what do we need to allocate to the system and what do we need in return?
   1.1 What do we want from the software package?
      1.1.1 What are the IT requirements e.g. compatibility?
      1.1.2 What does the sales team expect to get?
      1.1.3 How will we able to fit it in to our overall marketing processes?
      1.1.4 We must remember that the customer is the C in CRM
   1.2 What are the hardware requirements – do we need to upgrade?

2. Research the suppliers that potentially have suitable software/hardware to satisfy our needs
   2.1 Shortlist those suppliers we will offer to bid after more detailed research e.g. costs, testimonials, product limitations.

(Note that this is only the start of the structure for illustrative purposes and it may go down through many more levels until is broken down into discrete work packages. You may also note that the text that follows the diagram reflects the hierarchical structure of the diagram.)

The WBS will go down through a series of levels until the project tasks produce manageable outputs. These are called *work packages*. Work packages are normally viewed as being *deliverables* or products at the lowest level of the WBS. Deliverables are the tangible outputs from work, which are normally then signed off as complete. This may be a milestone – the end of a period of work.

Identifying the work packages forms the foundation for developing schedules, budgets and resource requirements, and also forms the foundation for assigning responsibilities.

Work packages can be split into activities or tasks that are used to create a workflow. These contrast with activities and tasks, which are about what is involved in doing work.

Figure 17.3 looks at the process that would be involved in the purchasing of the CRM software outlined in Figure 17.2. It considers a traditional purchasing of traditional physical goods with the alternative of buying software. Again, remember that it is included as an illustration, and you may very well see variations in your organisation.

Some people refer to the 80-hour rule to make the decision about the bottom level. The bottom level of a WBS should identify 80 hours or fewer of work. This WBS is the foundation for the other elements of the project plan. Theh project manager's mantra states that 'if it is not in the WBS, then it is not in the plan'. Clearly, there must be attention to this for the project to be successful, but you may well miss some issues if you are new to project management.

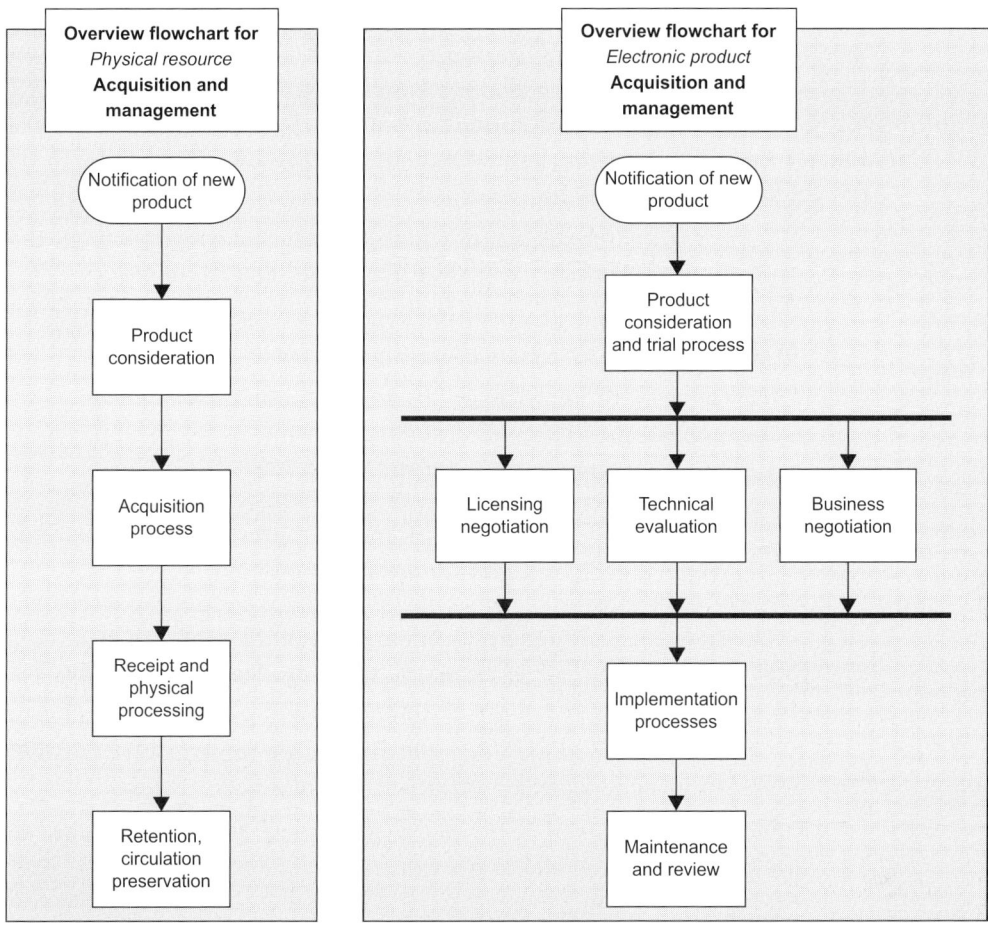

FIGURE 17.3   *Buying physical or electronic products*
Source: Resource Management Workflow Flowchart accessed 01/04/2009
http://www.library.cornell.edu/cts/elicensestudy/dlfdeliverables/fallforum2003/Workflow_final.doc

Seek advice from others to check that this is not a major issue.
Some key things to review concerning a WBS are:

- Does the WBS go outside the scope of the project?
- Does the WBS cover the entire scope of the project?
- Does the WBS ultimately result in deliverables?

ESTIMATING TIMING AND TASK DURATION

Project duration defines the length of time (in hours, days, weeks or months)
to complete an activity. Typically, in marketing projects, the deadline will be
set, such as to launch in time for a Christmas holiday or before the Olympics.

Working back from the set deadlines is stressful for a project manager, and often for all other members of the project team too.

Task and activity duration also needs to be determined for planning purposes. Estimating the task duration for work packages is one of the most difficult things for a novice project manager. There are several ways to try and determine this:

- Consider similar activities for which you have information about the task duration. However, this may not be possible for all tasks.

- Historical data may identify how long tasks or activities have taken in the past. However, some project tasks may be new tasks.

- Expert advice – or knowledge – from senior managers can give indications of the likely – or desired – outcomes.

Problems with establishing time periods include:

1. Lack of experience in planning time duration for tasks, and in doing activities.

2. Clearly, novices will typically take longer than experienced workers to do the same tasks, and may be unaware of the problems that take time. Clearly, lack of experience here can lead to unrealistic timescales.

3. Complexity of the marketing problems – often these involve creative tasks, for which focusing on time may detract from quality.

4. Unexpected events or delays due to illness etc. Also, mistakes or other problems can add to the time needed. Contingencies may have to be built into the systems.

5. Novices tend to underestimate the amount of work involved in any tasks. Expert project managers tend to use the longest predicted duration in scheduling, as this allows for possible delays.

There is a dual issue here. It is very difficult to judge the time taken for new projects or new activities or tasks. Some tasks involved in marketing activities – such as creative work – are especially difficult to do 'to a timescale'. This in turn will impact on the feasibility of the project completion date.

ACTIVITY 17.1

Many students underestimate the amount of time taken to undertake a project or dissertation. They look at the word count, compare this to an essay and then say 'I can write a 2000 word essay in 3 hours, so a dissertation of 10,000 words will take 15 hours'.

Is this the case? What assumptions underpin this? How valid are they?

DETERMINING REQUIREMENTS – A RESOURCE CHECKLIST

Project resourcing clearly varies depending on the type and size of projects. The central issue in identifying this is using the WBS and estimated timings to determine the resource requirements to complete the project on time and budget:

a. *The people* to be involved in the project, the level of their commitment, and the required level of skills.

b. *The facilities* for the project planning, and depending on the project, its implementation,

c. *The equipment* required, such as computers, cameras, or other audio-visual equipment.

d. *The money* – a budget needed to complete the task. There will often be an iterative process to determine budgets, taking account of the costs, timescales etc.

e. *The materials* – what tangibles, consumables or other items will be required in the process.

The resources need to be determined at this stage, and this becomes a reference point for monitoring resource use once the project starts. While the WBS tends to work top down, many argue that resources should be determined from the bottom up. Contingencies may need to be built in for some resources.

SEQUENCING WORK

The tasks so far have complexities, but the real difficulties in project planning come through scheduling. Scheduling is essentially about the links between and among activities/tasks and or people and organisations. Some work tasks will be completed in parallel, while others will be dependent on the completion of other activities.

Scheduling examines the sequence of tasks, both independent and interrelated, that will be undertaken. This is then organised into a series of subschedules and charts, which can be prepared from the master plan, detailing what will happen when, by whom, and detailing the interfaces and the milestones for the tasks.

For example, a brochure cannot be printed until the content has been prepared. The content cannot be prepared until a copywriter has been appointed and the R&D team has provided the product information. However, a printer can be sourced while the copy is being written.

Once you know what needs to be done, you need to examine the work involved to determine:

Predecessor tasks: those required for another task to be completed.
Successor tasks: those that cannot start until another task has been completed.

The schedule can be prepared once this workflow is established. The schedule becomes a key tool in managing progress.

ACTIVITY 17.2

A common example that is often used to identify predecessor tasks and successor tasks is one that starts with wanting to drink a cup of tea.

Choose a situation – either in the office or at home – and work through the individual steps involved in this process.

Detailed scheduling turns the project plan into action plans, on the basis of the WBS. Each WBS task is normally named and numbered, and the duration of tasks, any lead or lag times, and resources and budget involved must be estimated in order for a detailed schedule to be undertaken. Clearly, this reinforces the need for good time and resource estimates. Each WBS task should become the responsibility of a named individual.

However, schedules will often feature *ideal* start dates and *late* finish dates. Ideal start dates are the latest dates for an activity to start, if delays are to be avoided. Late finish dates are the latest dates for an activity to finish without causing delays in the project.

Later in the project, revised schedules are prepared as issues emerge. Rescheduling does not always result in delays in completion, as contingencies – for time or budget – may be built into the project plan. However, if the delays exceed this, and there is no flexibility with the delivery date or resources, terminating the project should be considered. Many tools are used to present schedules.

GANTT CHARTS

Schedules are commonly presented pictorially as Gantt charts, as these are easy to understand. This provides a graphical presentation of the information in the WBS. Each work package or activity has a row in the chart, with dates (days, weeks or months, depending on the project length) indicated along the top of the chart. The time allocated for each task is presented as a shaded area or bar, which spans the start and finish date of each task on the project. Work packages can be organised in roughly chronological order, although some are concurrent or overlap. The overall objective is to display and track progress towards project completion (Figure 17.4)

Visit the following website to see further examples of a Gantt chart, resource estimates and other information for a litter prevention campaign: (Source: http://www.ecy.wa.gov/pubs/0107043.pdf)

NETWORK ANALYSIS TOOLS

Network analysis tools show dependencies in work activities. Two common network analysis tools are CPM (Critical Path Methodology, often called Critical Path Analysis) and PERT (Program Evaluation and Review Technique). These techniques are commonly combined, as PERT/CPM. Their focus is on managing the total length of the project, rather than the time for each aspect of the project (like Gantt charts).

A path is a series of connected activities. Projects have several potential paths. The term critical path describes the sequence of activities that takes the longest total time required to complete the project. A delay in any activity in the critical path means that the project will face a delay.

PERT is used to determine how much time a project needs before it is completed, on the basis of activities being completed within a best, worst and most likely time estimate. An average time for completion is determined from the best, worst and most likely time estimates.

Project management software simplifies the preparation of these schedules – and revised schedules as the project continues. These can also be designed to show schedules for the whole project, or by task, person or date, so that these facilitate the project communications.

Later in the project, revised schedules are prepared as issues emerge. Rescheduling does not always result in delays in completion, as contingencies – for time or budget – may be built into the project plan. However, if the delays exceed this, and there is no flexibility with the delivery date or resources, terminating the project should be considered.

Although this may appear to some students to be far removed from marketing, these methods should not detrimentally affect the creative elements involved in building a campaign, but it should make sure that basic managerial functions such as setting target dates, monitoring progress and identifying potential problems are carried out rigorously.

P-R-O-J-E-C-T	2000			2001									R-E-S-P
	Oct	Nov	Dec	Jan	Feb	Mar	Apr	May	Jun	Jul	Aug	Sep	
ENGINEERING													ENGINEERING
Site Survey	18	15											Marwell Engineering
Draft Survey Results	18		4										Marwell Engineering
GMBH Review			4 · 29										Lost Creek Point Mgmt
Survey RPT (Final)				1 · 22									Electrical Contractor
GMBH RFV Approval			3		6								Lost Creek Point Mgmt
System Design					14	20							Marwell Engineering
HMBC Review						20	4						Electrical Contractor
Bid and Award							4	4					Marwell Engineering
Construction Support							27					5	Marwell Engineering
CONSTRUCTION													CONSTRUCTION
Buy Cable Conduit							24	16					Electrical Contractor
Install Cable								2	7				Electrical Contractor
Procure Hardware							24	21					A & J Security
Install Hardware								21	20				A & J Security
Deliver Console									9 · 11				A & J Security
Load Data									13	11			Lost Creek Point Mgmt.
Configure Software									1	26			A & J Security

FIGURE 17.4 Sample Gantt chart for an engineering project

Source: http://www.ganttchart.com/Chart/BasicGantt.pdf original chart was constructed using Milestones Software

RISK MANAGEMENT

Projects managers must address the levels of risk. You should refer to the chapters in this book specifically addressing this. However, the foundations of project risk management are summarised here.

THE PROJECT RISK MANAGEMENT PROCESS

1. Risk identification – have you identified the risks for the project, and the implications of these on the business?

2. Risk analysis – have you identified risks, and the chances of these affecting the time, cost, performance and outcomes of the project, and what the consequences of these risks are?

3. Risk planning – have you prepared contingency plans to avoid, address or minimise risks to the project achieving its time, cost and performance outcomes?

4. Risk monitoring – have you got a system in place to monitor these potential risks and to pick up on any other risks that might impact on the project process or outcomes?

PREPARING THE INTEGRATED PLANNING DOCUMENT

The above process helps identify the project planning document. Increasingly, project team members will not access a paper document, but use online packages, which are addressed in the next chapter.

However, the starting document often provides a useful snapshot of the starting position. There *will* be changes as the project develops. It is useful to understand how and why these occur.

This project plan is the key resource for measuring project performance.

SUMMARY

The terminology here can be a bit confusing if you are new to Project Management. However, the following summarises the most important elements from this section:

- Start the WBS from the top down, not bottom up.

- Identify all resources required for the project, and ensure that the budget addresses these.
- Assign responsibilities for each work package or activity.
- Identify concurrent activities.
- Examine and understand predecessor and successor tasks.
- Prepare and circulate schedules.

CHAPTER 18

Project Termination and Review

INTRODUCTION

Project termination is when work on the project is complete. Ideally, this should be when the project has reached its successful conclusion. Alternatively, it can be stopped when a project has problems or will fail to achieve the outcomes.

Termination clearly is at the end of a project life cycle (whether the expected end or a premature end), so activities at termination rarely impact on the success of the project. However, it can impact on the success of future projects and on attitudes to the terminated project and the project team.

Managing termination is therefore the final stage in effective project management. Project termination begins with the project termination decision (how to decide and whether to terminate). This is followed by the termination implementation process. Finally, once a project has been terminated, a project review will then take place, which will use evaluation tools to address the dimensions of success and failure. These topics are the focus of this chapter.

THE PROJECT TERMINATION DECISION

Two key models or forms of project decision making exist:

- Models based on the extent to which the project has achieved – or failed to achieve – its desired outcomes

- Models that compare the project against generally accepted standards for success and failure for a project

ASSESSING PROJECT TERMINATION

A project can be terminated at any stage in the project process. Whether projects should continue is essentially a resource allocation decision. Generally, this follows a project review, or results from other organisational decisions.

Meredith and Mantell (2003) state:

that the primary criterion for project continuance or termination is whether or not the organisation is willing to invest the estimated time and cost required to complete the project, given the project's current status and expected outcome.

They argue that this definition can be applied to all projects. In practice, some marketing managers allow tactical projects to continue, without substantial review, if there is no 'bad news' associated with them. A departmental plan will have a range of subprojects, such as those designed to support a new brand launch. Each element will normally continue – unless risk, budget or other factors go right out of control.

While project managers should be committed to their projects, they should also recognise when and how to stop unsuccessful projects. Often, project managers will protect their projects, because of an emotional involvement or concern over their careers. Early project termination can be emotional though, as reflected in the language used.

Projects that finish early are 'culled' or have 'hatchets' taken to them. In reality, continuing some projects may have worse outcomes on the careers of the managers and of the sponsoring organisation. Usually, project termination decisions are made by senior sponsors rather than project managers.

ACTIVITY 18.1

Marketing writer Philip Kotler said:

In a downturn, it can be common for a CEO to put the stoppers on marketing projects that are costing the company, as they want to save money. Along with R&D, marketing is often one of the first things to suffer.

(*Source*: The age of turbulence, *Business and Leadership* http://www.businessandleadership.com/marketing/news/article/12249/marketing/the-age-of-turbulence accessed at 26.01.2009)

For a valid project of your choice (i.e. one which you believe will achieve results), identify how you would defend your chosen project from being terminated.

CRITERIA FOR REVIEWING ONGOING PROJECT TERMINATION

Relatively little attention has been given to criteria for ongoing project termination in formal studies, and especially in marketing. Dean (1968) identified the following criteria for terminating a project early (Table 18.1):

- Low probability of technical/commercial success
- Low profitability/ROI/market potential
- Damaging cost growth
- Change in competitive factors/market needs
- Technical problems that cannot be resolved

- Competing projects having higher priority within the organisation or department
- Schedule delays

Despite the age of Dean's work, these issues remain valid. Note that Dean includes changing market situations, which is not explicitly mentioned in Meredith and Mantell's definition. Studies in 2008–2009 showed that that over 50% of US marketing managers were considering culling projects or project expenditure. It is not clear whether this is due to lower budgets, less cash to invest in marketing or changes in potential rewards from projects.

Organisations rarely have formal criteria for evaluating the early termination of projects. Often, it is easier – in terms of the level of investment and the external evidence of the project – to stop marketing projects than those with tangible evidence of work completed, for example construction projects. It is also easier to stop projects that do not have a full-time team as there are no redundancies. Notably, staff motivation and concerns are often not included in project termination decisions.

Table 18.1	Project termination criteria
Termination evaluation criteria	Possible tools for evaluation
Probability of technical/commercial success	Marketing research, profit/loss analysis, value analysis
Profitability/ROI/market potential	Marketing research, profit/loss analysis, value analysis
Cost growth	Budgeting, variance analysis
Changing competitive factors/market needs	Marketing intelligence, profit/loss analysis
Technical problems that cannot be resolved	Project viability, marketing mix analysis
Competing projects having higher priority within the organisation or department	Investment performance analysis, project priority review
Schedule delays	Variance analysis, impact on profit/loss

CASE EXAMPLE – Edinburgh

The City of Edinburgh decided to support a new £515 million tram system in 2007 after a period of debate and dispute. However, the work on the project caused major traffic problems from 2008 on, with central routes being at 'gridlock', and temporary traffic measures had not worked. Those who opposed the scheme called for the resignation of the CEO of the tram project company (TIE) in September 2008. A month later, he resigned for personal reasons.

In February 2009, chaos again hit Edinburgh's traffic, when work on the famous Princes Street was due to start. TIE said that the dispute arose because contractors were in dispute over 'additional costs', which TIE said would add over £50 million to the project budget.

The time delays are of major concern to local retailers, who lobbied over the scheduling of this work in order to ensure that the work was completed before the Christmas holiday shopping period.

Review Meredith and Mantell's definition of the project termination decision, and Dean's criteria for evaluating project termination. What is the chance that this project will be terminated as a result? What does this demonstrate about project termination decisions?

As Activity 18.2 shows, the decision to end a project is complex. This is particularly the case in marketing projects, where the project is not just measured on the activity, but also on the outcomes that the implementation of the project achieves. Expectations of the outcomes may well exist, but these may not be easily transferred between projects.

For example, commonly, companies will have a facility to share models of successful marketing communications activities (i.e. share knowledge). This can be through manuals, handbooks, videos or conference presentations. Some campaigns may well have achieved success in the past, but these may not apply in future:

- New competitor campaigns may be better.
- Customers may already be aware of the communications approach.
- Customer budgets may be cut.
- The new product may not be as relevant as those in the past.

More sophisticated organisations will use decision support systems to decide on project termination. This is similar to the initial project choice review, considering a range of projects on a predetermined range of factors. Managers should specify thresholds to determine which projects should face more specific review.

Some projects die through even though there is no formal decision to stop the project, usually because work is no longer being undertaken.

Project progress has slowed down so much that the project is no longer active. Sometimes, this is due to the members of the project team moving on to 'more interesting topics', or even the project manager moving to other work.

The project is no longer achieving the level of resourcing (people and budget) required enabling progress. This could be the result of the project no longer being considered a high priority, because of company budgetary constraints, or even the project champion no longer getting top-level management support.

IMPLEMENTATION OF PROJECT TERMINATION

By definition, a project will eventually be terminated once it has achieved its outcomes and is no longer required. Examples of this would be the launch of the new product or the implementation of a new communications plan.

Projects – irrespective of whether they are culled prematurely or finish along their expected course – can be:

- Following a planned and structure process
- Sudden, and without any warning or support

In many cases, the project manager's final responsibility is to complete the project review. The project review is to detail the lessons learnt and the outcomes of the project. However, without full budgeting and scheduling of this activity, it may not happen. Often, organisations forget the value of learning from the project experience, despite increasing commitment to ideas of 'learning from success' or defining themselves as 'learning organisations'.

Project termination decisions consider many aspects that are part of the project process. In minor projects, many of these will be irrelevant. In others, they will be key factors for future project success.

Key termination tasks include:

1. *Personnel issues*, which will differ depending on the type of project organisation. In project team organisation, some team members will need help in finding new jobs and in disengaging from the project and project issues. This can also apply to external parties – the loss of a major advertising account can impact on personnel who have been heavily involved in projects for that customer.

2. *Operations/Logistics/Manufacturing*, which will change post-project, when this moves to general activity. Support specialists in these functions may return to general management and not focus on issues related to the project. Often, support and training issues to ensure success in practice.

3. *Accounting and Financial* matters need to be 'closed'. The project budget and expenditure need to be audited or verified and signed off. Any balances (positive or negative) need to be addressed.

4. *Processes* will need to be clearly specified and operationalised. For example, compliance issues will need to be clearly specified with appropriate training briefs for their implementation in a new financial product. This may require specification for all new procedures.

5. *Information Systems* are closely related to other processes. However, data protection issues may require more attention to personal details, and examination of personal data into internal systems.

6. *Marketing activities*, both internal and external, should be verified as in alignment with the project outcomes.

CASE EXAMPLE

A B2B manufacturer set in place a project to develop and launch a website for its partners (i.e. intermediaries), which would offer a range of information, administration and support activities. The intention was to move the partners away from more labour-intensive forms of dealer support, which would enable the partners to give better service to their customers. The project budget was set at the cost of running a call centre for handling partner enquiries and support over a two-year period. The cost-saving was to be split between the manufacturer and its trade partners. Therefore, moving to this new website, once developed, would improve channel margins.

The website development went through several stages of development, such as specification, routing, content development and testing. The initial testing involved mirroring a sample of queries managed through the dealer support call centre. Beta testing of the site amongst selected partners was put in place, with pop-up questionnaires, observations and discussions to review their site usage, attitudes etc.

Modifications were made to the process, and the full-scale launch of the project was signed off into the mainstream company activity within the original time schedule.

ACTIVITY 18.3

Refer to the partners' website launch case history above.
    Was this project a success?

THE PROJECT REPORT

At the end of the project, two differing views of the project report exist:

1. Project report identifying the success of the project
2. Project history to encourage learning

A Project Success Report focuses on the outcomes of the project, and should identify:

a. Whether the project's objectives have been met and identifying the success of the project on the basis of this
b. A comparison of the performance against the planned target time and cost
c. Whether the original project plan needed changes
d. Analysis of any changes to time, cost, outcomes, during the project
e. Any other organisational requirements, e.g. staff performance, testing etc.

CASE EXAMPLE – Millennium Dome

The Millennium Dome was a one-off event to celebrate the 2000 Millennium. After opening on New Year's Eve, 1999, it would remain open to the public throughout 2000 only. The project funding was from three sources: the UK National Lottery, paying visitors and commercial sponsors. It was built and managed by the New Millennium Experience Company, which was fully owned by the UK government. A senior civil servant managed the development of the Dome and operations.

The opening date of 31 December, 1999 was critical to the success of this project. A second target was for sponsorship income of £175 million, to be invested in 14 zones of the Millennium Dome. A third target was the 12 million visitors required to fund the Dome during its year of operation.

Adverse publicity about the project began months before its opening, with doubts that the Dome would be ready in time and comments on the lack of heating and the poor quality of some sponsored exhibits.

The opening event went ahead as scheduled and was televised live. The UK media carried extensive coverage of well-known invited guests being left standing outside for hours in adverse weather owing to a ticketing problem, rather than the entertainment.

The overoptimistic commercial sponsorship target created problems with the quantity and quality of the exhibits. The media reported that there was less display and interactivity than was expected.

After opening to the public, the paying visitor numbers were below forecast, which reduced revenue. By mid-2000, accountants were asked to review the financial situation of the Dome, who determined the project was financially unsound. Major changes were made, including the appointment of a new Chief Executive to lead the Dome.

By July 2000, the number of visitors had surpassed the 1999 top visitor numbers for a UK 'pay-to-visit' attraction. A visitor survey found visitor satisfaction to be 87%.

Source: On the basis of information from The National Audit Commission, The Millennium Dome, Report by the Comptroller and Auditor General, HC 936 Session 1999–2000: 9 November 2000, available at http://www.nao.org.uk/publications/nao_reports/9900936es.pdf

The Project Success Report can be an important way of showing stakeholders that the project has achieved its outcomes, or identifying the reasons for failure. This is critical for the project manager's future career.

The Project History focuses on 'lessons learned' for future projects, rather than on the merits of the project. This report is sometimes called a project history. This history will examine the following to determine what worked and what did not, and when and why problems occurred.

It will address:

Project performance – the outcomes, successes, failures and challenges

Administrative performance – reports and reporting, communications and meetings, review procedures, scoping and change procedures, financial management

Project organisation – how this changed throughout the project, and how this helped or hindered the project

Project teams – how this performed, recommendations for future teams

Project management – scoping, plans, methodologies, budgets, schedules, risk management etc.

Table 18.2	Summary of project history		
	What went well	**What went badly**	**Recommendations**
Project performance			
Admin performance			
Project organisation			
Project teams			
Project management			

Often, these reviews will be presented in a meeting or presentation. Simply, this basic finding can be summarised in a presentation, and Table 18.2 will help identify these key issues.

More formal project audits are often undertaken for major projects, and especially those in the public sector.

ACTIVITY 18.4

Refer to the Millennium Dome case and answer the following questions.

1. Who were the stakeholders for the Millennium Dome, and what did they seek?
2. What was the project management life cycle for the Millennium Dome project?
3. Was the Millennium Dome project a success or a failure? Why?

Often, organisations do not require these reports despite their contribution to project management knowledge and future projects. Often, other priorities overtake this, or the project manager has moved to other projects or has a wish to move on. Further, on longer projects, there is much documentation, but often the reasons for changes or problems are not noted.

SUMMARY

We have looked at the termination of projects and understand that this can be at full completion or earlier.

We have looked at the criteria to help decide if an early termination is beneficial.

We understand that companies may not always follow the path that the logical review indicates.

We understand what the key termination tasks are and what importance they have.

We have looked at the use of the project report for the termination stage.

CHAPTER 19

Methodologies

INTRODUCTION

This may be a difficult chapter for some students. You are getting involved in topics that are central to professional project managers. Evaluating project methodologies can be complex and it is best done considering a specific project. The content here is rather descriptive of the options.

However, as the assessment for this module is an applied assignment, you should reflect on the methodologies used by your organisation and the relative characteristics, strengths and weaknesses of the different methodologies. You should also take time to see demonstrations or read about the application of different approaches as these may introduce you to new – and appropriate – approaches. Weblinks are included in this chapter, but you should also use your own research to find out about other project methodologies.

Managing people is not a major aspect of this part of the syllabus, as it is covered in the Managing Marketing module. However, this chapter adds a few pointers about some specifics of managing people in projects.

KEY DEFINITIONS

Project management methodology	A documented process for management of projects that contains procedures, definitions and roles and responsibilities.
Process methodologies	Process methodologies are those that define at the start, the processes to be followed in the project.
Agile methodologies	Agile methodologies are those that enable changes to projects following review stages in the project.
Project management competencies	Project management competencies are the capability to undertake project management processes in a professional and successful manner.

On completion of this chapter, you should not expect to be an expert in project management methodologies, but rather, you should be aware of different alternatives, and be prepared to consider alternatives. You should be aware of some of the competencies needed to overcome problems and successfully manage people within projects.

Project management methodologies, with frameworks, tools and guidelines, provide structure and guidance for the project's implementation.

Organisations use methodologies to help ensure that the project is planned and controlled well, that there is clear understanding of the project process and WBS and that risks and resources are managed. Adopting a methodology for the organisation will ensure that people have the shared knowledge of the language and systems for project management within the organisation.

Choosing the right methodology is matching the suitability of a given methodology to:

- The size and complexity of the project
- The project risk levels
- The desired outcomes of the project
- The skills and abilities of the project manager and team members

Some organisations may have internal operations manuals, explaining the stages of managing a project. This is a simple form of methodology. Increasingly, the discussion of project management methodologies is linked to the use of computer software, and methodologies and software are commonly closely linked.

PROJECT MANAGEMENT METHODOLOGIES

Project management approaches vary substantially, across a continuum, with the following extremes:

Organisations have no formal methodology, which means that the project manager has all the information and plans. Team members may be less involved or committed because they lack information. Management may be given only limited information on progress, as reporting takes time.

An organisation-wide methodology is applied for all projects and departments. Usually, this is a sophisticated methodology, which prepares plans, metrics, communications tasks etc. Often, these methodologies require training for all participants. However, an overly complex methodology may be cumbersome for some projects, such as simple, 'soft' or creative projects, and may demotivate people.

Between these extremes, there are many off-the-shelf software packages for managing projects, including Microsoft Project. Typically, these require some training, but are not the highly specialist project management methodologies. These packages identify the core processes and reporting that is required in project management, and can be bought or licensed for application. Pre-established packages are cheaper than the specialist packages. They may increase project management efficiency by automating planning and reporting processes. In turn, this improves effectiveness, such as reducing risks.

These packages are flexible enough to take account of a project's unique aspects. These can be customised for marketing projects, but there are also 'off-the-shelf' software packages specifically for marketing projects.

A second option is to buy an existing methodology and customise it (or have it customised) for a specific situation. This is generally for more sophisticated projects and project-focused organisations. There is a fine line here between the adaptation of an existing methodology and the development of in-house methodologies, customised for an organisation's skills, values and best practices. The latter are becoming less common with ever-increasing numbers of quality project management software. Sophisticated customised packages are typically time consuming and expensive, and staff must be trained to use these.

Use a search engine such as Google to identify different project management software packages for marketing, and investigate these further. These could include:

http://www.office.microsoft.com/en-gb/FX010857951033.aspx

This Microsoft Office Project package details its key benefits, gives you the chance to see a demonstration and also to download this for a 60-day free trial. If you do not know any other package, you might like to plan your assessment for this module on this package. (But remember the 60-day limit, if your company does not have a license for this!)

www.vertabase.com/tour1.html

This software offers a quick tour of the highlights of the software, and also offers a trial. There is detailed information on product features, including various reports. Also check out the case studies for insight.

http://www.wrike.com/

This is an online project management service, and offers the product features, free demonstration and also case studies and testimonials. Interestingly, this software works directly with email systems to ensure better team collaboration. It also specifically targets marketing professionals and products.

http://www.projectminder.com/

The site makes available software for project management that is focused on vertical markets, including consultancies and agencies. This is very strongly focused on managing time and cost. This site has interesting white papers for those in these sectors. It also offers a small business version.

CASE EXAMPLE

The importance of Project Management as a function, and specifically of the use of Project Management Methodologies, is evident in a recent survey of Irish companies.

The survey found that a specific project management methodology was defined in 75% of respondents, which was 15% increase from that in 2007.

This may be related to the growth in project management departments, which now exist in more than half of the respondent companies (54% – an increase of 8ᵛ% from 2007).

Interestingly, the greatest proportional increase was in the use of management tools for project performance, which rose from 9% in 2007 to 21% in 2008. However, this growth is probably a function of increased pressure on accountability on schedules and cost, and the increasing focus on risk management. It is likely to increase further in the future.

(*Source*: Anon (2008) AddedMETRICS. *PM Network*, 22(9), 22.)

ACTIVITY 19.1

Check out the use of a specific project management methodology in your organisation.

What do your results suggest about your organisation's approach to project management?

CORE PROJECT MANAGEMENT METHODOLOGIES

Using existing methodology is increasingly common, especially in larger organisations that have extensive project management experience. Often, job advertisements for projects managers detail the methodology to be used, and ask for experience in using this technology.

This discussion presents features of two common process methodologies:

1. PRINCE/PRINCE2
2. Scalable methodology

Process methodologies are those that follow a formal planning stage, whereby processes are determined for undertaking the project.

PRINCE/PRINCE2

PRINCE (PRojects INControlled Environments) methodologies are commonly used in public sector project management, although they were originally designed for developing and implementing information systems.

It is the default methodology for public sector organisations in the United Kingdom, and is widely used by large organisations across Europe. A related approach is Managing Successful Programmes (MSP). Both approaches are structured, but adaptable to different projects and programmes.

PRINCE methodologies have:

- A clear management structure
- Formal allocation of project roles and responsibilities
- Plans for resourcing and technical issues
- Control procedures
- A focus on products – deliverables to the customer and project deliverables for the management of the project

PRINCE methodologies have three separate progress assurance roles:

1. *The business*– The Business Assurance Coordinator (BAC) ensures that the project meets the organisation's mission.

2. *The specialist*– The Technical Coordinator is responsible for ensuring that the project does not have technical problems.

3. *The user*– The User Assurance Coordinator represents the user throughout the process.

These different roles ensure that the various stakeholders agree that the project is satisfactory (in terms of the cost, quality and delivery) from all perspectives.

In terms of progress planning and monitoring, PRINCE2 shows:

- The project life-cycle stages
- Progress against plan and key user-defined decision points
- Alerts for any variance from plan

In addition, PRINCE2 enables:

- Management and stakeholder involvement at critical times in the project

- Effective communication within the project team and other stakeholders

However, PRINCE2 has its critics, who claim it will:

- Make projects longer
- Increase project costs
- Tie up resources
- Delay payback on the project
- Increase risks of failure

Read more information on PRINCE2 at www.prince2.com/.

SCALABLE METHODOLOGY

Scalable methodology recognises the differences in project size, risk and complexity, and allows a customised best practice management approach for each project. This approach builds on the Project Management Institute's PMBOK (Project Management Body of Knowledge), identifying differences between minor and major projects on nine dimensions and their impact on project management.

Managers can mix 'n' match to develop an appropriate project approach, on the basis of consideration of the issues in Table 19.1.

CASE EXAMPLE – GE and 3M

3M's focus on innovation has become almost legendary – the stories of the development of Post-it-Notes and Scotchguard are widely cited as examples of the company's supportive environment for innovation. However, 3M's performance began to wane in the eyes of its investors. In late 2000, a new Chief Executive Officer was appointed to introduce new business practices to the company. James McNerney, who had worked in several divisions of GE (General Electric) in the United States and Asia, was 3M's first CEO from outside the company.

Traditionally, 3M and GE had different management approaches. GE has strong management control and operating processes managed from the centre, while 3M allowed staff to have discretion in their workload as a way of stimulating innovation. *Fortune* (2002) characterised the different management approaches in GE and 3M as 'GE gave its managers a toolbox; 3M functioned more like a sandbox'.

McNerney's early changes at 3M focused on what he learned and applied at GE.

Sources: Useem, J. (2002) Jim McNerney thinks he can turn 3M from a good company into a great one – with a little help from his former employer, General Electric, *Fortune*, 8 December, 146(3).

Business Week Online (2004) The Best & Worst Managers of 2003 – The Best Managers – James McNerney, 3M, January 12, accessed at www.businessweek.com/magazine/content/04_02/b3865711.htm, www.3m.com

ACTIVITY 19.2

Refer to the GE and 3M case on the following page and answer the following questions.

What does the comment that 'GE gave its managers a toolbox; 3M functioned more like a sandbox' suggest about how projects might be managed in GE and 3M?

How easily would the above formal project management processes fit with the existing 3M and GE corporate cultures?

Table 19.1	Key issues and areas for adaptation in scalable methodology

Integration – project initiation and management issues, such as project charters, project stakeholders and project life-cycle phases and milestones for different sizes of projects

Scope – requirements definition, scope control and work breakdown structure for different sizes of projects

Time – managing, estimating and tracking schedules and critical path management for different projects

Cost – approaches for cost estimating, budgeting and control for different projects

Quality – different quality requirements (project output) to ensure customer satisfaction from different projects

Risk – means of identifying, evaluating and responding to risks in the project and its environment

Human resources – leadership, staffing, organisation and team building for different sizes of projects

Communications – management actions required to ensure effective communication on different sizes of projects and project teams

Procurement – how to manage acquisitions and contract administration to manage project costs, schedules and quality risks

Source: Adapted from www.hyperthot.com/pm_intro.htm

AGILE METHODOLOGIES

A change in recent years has come about owing to criticisms of the process-driven methodologies (such as PRINCE2 and scalable methodology) because they lacked the capacity to adapt as the project developed. New agile methodologies were developed, which allow the project to adapt to changes in the changing environment and business challenges. Although they are seen as contrasting with the process methodologies, they are actually considered to be 'half-way' between a process methodology and no methodology.

Agile methodologies are defined as being:

Adaptive rather than predictive– Agile approaches welcome changes, rather than have fixed plans.

Focused on people rather than process– Process methods focus the process set, and anyone could implement the plans. Agile approaches recognise that people have skills that can add to the project as it progresses.

- Adaptive Project Framework (ADF)

ADF is a customer-focused methodology, which is based on being:

- Client focused and client-driven
- Frequent and early results reporting

- Focused on questioning and introspection
- Change is good, when it is moving to a better solution

ADF allows project scope to vary within defined time and cost levels. The project scope is reviewed in several iterations, by involving the client in identifying the issues that are of most value to the business. This means that the project changes course to deliver the maximum business value.

This approach was developed for IT projects, after many of them failed to deliver using the traditional and more rigid methodologies. However, its focus and flexibility make it appropriate for marketing projects.

ACTIVITY 19.3

This approach breaks one of the cardinal rules of good project management – that of defining and managing scope. Does this mean that scope definition is not an important activity?

CHOOSING A METHODOLOGY

The choice of a project methodology of commonly set given the preferences of the commissioning organisation. However, if you have an open choice of methodology, you should consider the following issues to make an informed choice:

- Availability of software
- Number of members of the team
- Team member communications
- Complexity of the task
- Training required to effectively utilise the methodology
- Cost of the methodology to acquire or use

SUMMARY

The way in which a project is planned and managed is referred to as the project methodology. Project methodologies vary in sophistication and in structure. Many methodologies are now based on computer software, which enables sharing of information. Some organisations have preferred methodologies, which then dictate the process for project management. In others, a choice of methods may be available. Project managers should identify an appropriate methodology for the project.

The traditional project management methodologies are usually process methodologies, but increasing attention is being given to agile methodologies that may change some aspects of the project scope as the work proceeds.

CHAPTER 20

Monitoring and Control

INTRODUCTION

At all stages of a project, activities need to be monitored. Targets should have been established as part of the project plan, but progress against these must be measured. Control mechanisms must exist that will allow corrective actions to occur if there is a substantial deviation from that which was projected.

KEY DEFINITIONS

Project monitoring	'Monitoring is the collecting, recording and reporting information concerning any and all aspects of project performance that the project manager or others in the organization which to know', Meredith and Mantell (2000).
Project control	'Control is the last element in the implementation cycle of planning- monitoring- controlling. .... In essence, control is the act of reducing the difference between plan and reality', Meredith and Mantell (2000).

Some project managers acknowledge that a perfect plan cannot exist. Plans are implemented in a fast-moving environment, with a range of inter-related activities and participants. Given that change is inevitable, then the project manager's role is to monitor progress to direct and enable to ensure that the project continues to make progress. If it is not making the progress intended, it is the project manager's responsibility to manage the project control by making adjustments to the plan.

This chapter focuses on monitoring and control. These terms are commonly 'unified', but are actually separate issues. Accordingly, these two separate terms become the structure for this chapter.

Objective measures of progress on performance are essential to realise project objectives and outcomes. These should be in the project document.

PROJECT MONITORING

Marketers are familiar with the concept of a planning and control cycle. Planning and control is different within the project environment from the analysis, planning, implementation and control cycle in marketing. Project managers focus on planning, monitoring and controlling. Planning was addressed earlier, and so now the focus moves to the monitoring phase.

According to Meredith and Mantell (2000):

> *Monitoring is the collecting, recording and reporting information concerning any and all aspects of project performance that the project manager or others in the organization wish to know.*

Tracking and monitoring progress helps to ensure an effective and efficient project, by reviewing project implementation against the approved plan and budget. Monitoring focuses on tracking data about activities and progress. It needs to be built on a good plan and substantial data. The design of a realistic chain of results, outcomes, outputs and activities is particularly important.

Monitoring cannot make a project successful – it is a 'neutral' part of the project process. However, timely monitoring (followed by effective control) can help identify – and avoid if necessary – the three Cs that challenge projects:

- Crises
- Catastrophes
- Change

Monitoring is usually the responsibility of the project coordinator and may be carried out informally (through weekly briefs) or through routine review of the project documents. The minimum forms of review for a project should be on the 'triple constraints' or:

- Time (schedule)
- Cost (budget) and
- Performance

Within this, the key parameters are:

- Current project status
- Progress to date

THE PROJECT MONITORING SYSTEM

The key stages in designing a monitoring system are:

- Identify the information requirements
- Identifying the key factors to be monitored
- Identifying the boundaries

Project monitoring normally relies on the parent organisation having a robust internal information system for monitoring and control.

The project monitoring system needs to be specified at the project initiation. Typically, this will look at the data collection process, the standards and the performance criteria. Unfortunately, these may change over time, because of changes affecting scope, legal changes or other budgetary or business priorities.

The monitoring system should also consider project milestones of performance criteria (such as the number of changes to plan or variations in resources usages).

The project action plan, WBS system and the further more detailed subplans are the reference for this. These describe the project activities, tasks, schedules, resource levels and costs for all elements. However, these factors may not identify all elements needed for project monitoring. Indeed, focusing on monitoring activity, rather than the output, is a common error. A project may have a considerable amount of activity, but the output may still be hidden. Focusing on the activity may mask the problems in creating output.

ACTIVITY 20.1

Using the indicators in the text above, identify factors that should be measured but which may not be part of the activity plans.

Once monitoring requirements are set, the data and information sources must be identified. Depending on how the project is being managed (i.e. as a self-contained project or organisation-wide), this may involve accessing a range of different data sources. The generic data requirements are:

- Project management data
- Operating data, including resource levels and usage
- Accounting and financial data
- Customer research
- Sponsor research

The monitoring system should then analyse this data to examine the progress of the project on various dimensions. At the most general level, these are looking to identify:

- What is going well, looking at the 'triple constraints' of progress, costs and resource utilisation.
- What is not going well, on similar dimensions.

Reporting Progress

The above material has identified various ways of monitoring progress, but these analyses are not only for the project manager. Commonly, monitoring is communicated to others through reports and meetings. Reports can be prepared by the project team, or prepared by independent auditors, depending on the organisation, type of project and the level of project risk. The reports will also form the record on which the project history will be based. However, the project manager has the ultimate responsibility for defining how reports and meetings are managed.

Project Status Reports

Project status reports provide updates on the project status.

Routine reports are normally those that provide updates on the project status.

- *An executive status report*, for the project sponsors or other key stakeholders who are not directly involved in the project activities. These should be prepared on an agreed schedule, often monthly or quarterly, and timed to fit with meetings with executive stakeholders. The focus of this report should be on the 'top-level' issues affecting progress and plans.

- *Project progress status reports* will be prepared on a regular time schedule. Projects with full-time team members or working within a tight schedule will commonly have these prepared weekly. Part-time projects may have a less frequent reporting schedule, as long as they do not have a short time duration.

Project status reports are normally prepared by those in key roles in the project team. These keep the project manager and project team up to date with progress or problems, and enable all to be aware of plans to reduce problems or recover from problems.

Extending Knowledge

You can find templates for project status reports on Microsoft's website. More specific reports are:

- *Exception reports*, prepared only for specific members of the project team involved in a key area under review or change. They are also prepared when there has been a change in the project, which has to be communicated to the project team. Some managers produce these to 'cover themselves' in case of later problems.

– *Special analysis reports* communicate the findings of a particular tool or activity, and where there may be learning that can be shared within the project or beyond. This is a form of 'working paper' or 'white paper' on that topic.

Independent Reviews or Project Audits

Independent reviews may be required on a periodic basis throughout the project. This is especially common in large or complex projects, but can be applied in smaller, risky projects.

These reviews or audits focus on the implementation process, ensuring that the project plans are being followed. They also examine how problems or variations are being managed.

Project Meetings

Internal software commonly encourages written reporting, but often reports are presented verbally at project meetings. Project meetings may be face-to-face or using video conferencing. Attendees can be project team members, subteam members or senior management. Project sponsors can question and direct the team if required.

Other specialist forms of meetings are outcome groups, with groups focusing on specific outcomes (e.g. on time delivery, late delivery). Focus groups may also be used as a form of listening mechanism to better understand progress dimensions. (This may become part of the balanced scorecard evaluation later.)

Monitoring Measures

Monitoring reviews the entire project and the individual tasks within it. The major monitoring tools are:

ACTIVITY 20.2

For your project, identify how you propose to report your project, taking account of the parties' need for information, and for sharing information. This should be weighed against the costs and time involved in the meetings.

- Progress checks
- Variance analysis
- Earned value analysis

Several forms of subsequent analysis are based on these. These are part of the control process.

Progress Checks

The most common forms of assessing progress are:

- Progress according to plan generally.

- Progress according to work packages or 'incremental milestones', which record the achievement of a critical element in the progress. For example, agreeing to the wording of a questionnaire in a marketing research project, which would enable the fieldwork to begin.

Variance Analysis

Variance analysis focuses on examining differences (or variances) between variables (e.g. time, cost, labour) on predetermined criteria. A marketing example of variance analysis is the actual sales against planned sales. Project managers monitor the progress of the project against schedule, or the expenditure of the project against target.

Variance analysis often starts by looking for deviations in top-level performance, which then starts a more detailed form of analysis. This is discussed further in the section 'Project control'.

Earned Value Analysis and Monitoring

Earned value (EV) is a measure of the performance to cost and schedule for a project. This is essentially about comparing expenditure against budgets (commonly called the 'baseline').

Earned value analysis (EVA) is a quantitative project management monitoring tool. This analysis is central to later project analysis.

EVA compares the costs and progress of elements of work against the budgeted costs and planned activities from the WBS. EVA is used routinely to monitor progress and predict project results.

EVA requires the following information:

- Planned Value (PV) (or the planned spend of the work). Some managers refer to this measure as Budgeted Cost of Work Scheduled (BCWS).

- Actual cost (AC) is what has been spent on the work undertaken until or at a given point in the life of a project.

- Earned value (EV) is the percentage of total project budget at a given point in the life cycle. Managers refer to this as the budgeted cost of work performed (BCWP). This is determined by the progress (as a percentage of the task) multiplied by the budgeted cost of work scheduled.

Many projects do not have a meaningful quantitative progress measure. For example, identifying quantitative measures for creative work, such as concept development being at a certain percentage level of completion, is difficult. Typically, tasks owners are asked to estimate progress, providing a subjective estimate of progress. However, this limitation can be managed by asking others to give their opinions of progress.

Typically, a project's EVA is presented in a chart of the earned value. Various measures (considered under the section 'Control') can be shown on such charts.

ACTIVITY 20.3

A work package for a new product launch was training the sales force to demonstrate the new product.

If there are 300 sales people, and 93 of these have been trained, and a total budget of £60,000 (PV) for this task, what is the earned value (EV) for this work package?

The actual cost (AC) is £24,000. Is this a problem?

OUTCOME MATRICES

Outcome matrices are diagrams that display influencing factors (predictors or inputs) and outcomes (results or benefits). These are best suited to projects where many factors interrelate, which is common in marketing projects. Mathematical models examine these interrelationships in great detail, but a simple diagram that shows the different interrelationships is sufficient for this qualification.

Developing this involves three stages:

1. Identify dimensions of outcomes that may be affected by other factors.
2. Identify influencing factors and inputs.
3. Match the influencing factors to the outcomes. (These can be ranked if required.)

Variations on this can examine outcomes for different market segments, using different communications approaches, or resources. The visual presentation helps classify resources and activities and identify any gaps in provision.

As these are monitoring tools, the content of these matrices should be updated regularly. Two alternative approaches to outcome matrices are presented in Table 20.1.

ACTIVITY 20.4

Complete Table 20.1 to add the details for the 'success of the promotional plan' criteria for a project in your organisation.

Table 20.1	Outcome matrix (project control)			
Outcome	**Success criteria**	**Data sources**	**Project factors affecting success**	**Non-project factors affecting success**
Launch of new product	Product available meeting time, cost and performance data	Project reports, including budgets, schedules, market research and product tests	Materials cost, labour availability, budget available	Competitor action, economic situations
Success of promotional plan				

PROJECT CONTROL

This section moves to the final part of the project implementation cycle control. Meredith and Mantell (2000) state that:

'control is the act of reducing the difference between plan and reality'.

The monitoring and control processes may be virtually seamless in some areas, such as reporting, analysing variance and then making corrective action plans to address the problems. However, the focus of the control stage moves from data monitoring to managerial insight and actions. Meredith and Mantel (2000) state the fundamental objectives of control to be:

'the regulation of results through the alteration of activities' and 'The stewardship of organizational assets'.

Most attention goes on the first of these. However, marketers cannot ignore the second, as it includes brand and reputation, as well as the organisation's human, physical and financial resources.

ACTIVITY 20.5

Read the case study on the following page. What are the consequences for Danone of this fight with Wahaha?

USING VARIANCE ANALYSIS IN CONTROL

Use of variance analysis extends beyond monitoring performance. It helps in:

- Future planning, based on learning from factors that have caused problems
- Management performance (levels of successes and failures)

CASE EXAMPLE

Chinese company Wahaha formed a joint venture (JV) with Hong Kong company Bai Fu Qin and French multinational Danone. In the JV, the latter two companies held 51% stake of a company called Jin Jia Investment. While Danone felt it (and its partner) had the majority stake, the Chairman of the Wahaha (Zong, reputed to be the wealthiest person in China) group felt that it was the majority partner in the JV. Wahaha transferred its brand to the JV (but not its cash), and exploited this. It was reported that a sales company used its staff to sell non-JV products alongside JV products.

Danone subsequently took over Bai Fu Qin's share of the business, giving it 51% of the JV, and claimed that Wahaha were using the brand name to sell projects that are not JV products. Danone sued its partner to gain ownership of the JV brand (Wahaha).

Initially, the legal case started in Sweden, as defined in the JV agreement. In 2007, a Chinese court ruled against Danone, largely based on the timing of the legal case. In 2009, a US court ruled that this should be decided in China.

Sources: Several online sources, including S.M. Dickinson (2007), http://www.chinaeconomicreview.com/cer/2007_09/Danone_v_Wahaha.html"Danone v. Wahaha", accessed on 01/04/09

Variance analysis is often used as a form of 'management by exception', where managers investigate where a deviation exists between the actual and planned schedule, performance or cost. Identifying acceptable levels of deviations in advance is important, so that focus can be given to those outside normal acceptable levels.

Once exceptional variations are identified, the causes or factors that contribute to the variation must be identified. A failure to achieve a new product launch date could then involve identifying the various factors that may have led to this. The process of identifying the various parts is known as decomposition.

Cost Measurement

Cost measurement of projects focuses on:

- *Cost Variance* – addresses variations in the actual cost of the project budget.

    Cost variance (CV) = Earned value (EV) – Actual cost (AC).

    A negative value for the cost variance shows that the project cost is falling below plan.

- *Cost Performance Index (CPI)*– an index for monitoring costs in projects over time.

    Cost performance index (CPI) = Earned value (EV)/Actual cost (AC).

    A CPI less than 1 indicates that the project is below plan. For example, a CPI of 0.75 shows that only 75 pence of earned value was achieved for every pound spent. A CPI of less than 1 and a negative CV indicate that the project cost performance is below the plan.

Schedule Measurement

Scheduling measurement follows a similar pattern to cost measurement:

- *Schedule Variance* evaluates the variance from the project schedule.

  Schedule variance (SV) = Earned value (EV) – Planned value (PV).

  A positive value (i.e. more than 1) for the schedule variance shows that more work was undertaken than was planned.

- *Schedule Performance Index* develops an index

  (SPI) = Earned value (EV)/Planned value (PV).

  An SPI value of more than 1 shows that more work was completed than planned. That is, an SPI of 1.25 shows that £1.25 of work value was actually undertaken for every £1 spent. An SPI greater than 1 and a positive SV indicate that more work was accomplished than was planned.

Watch when using schedule measurements though. Positive results do not necessarily say that you will complete the project ahead of schedule. The project schedule (e.g. the critical path) is the way to assess whether the work is completing to schedule.

ACTIVITY 20.6

For the sales training example above, calculate the Cost Performance Index (CPI).
Two months later, 150 of the 300 sales people have been trained. The actual costs have risen to £33,000.
Does the CPI suggest that the cost of this task is under control or going out of control?

Using Analysis to Forecast Budgets

The CPI can also be used as an input to forecast the likely project cost. Key analyses are:

- *Estimate to Complete* (ETC), which identifies the additional cost expected to complete the project.

- *Estimate at Completion* (EAC), which identifies the total cost of the project, on the basis of the completion of the existing project plan and the forecast expenditure.

On the basis of these measures, managers can prepare a further index measure – the *To Complete Performance Index* (TCPI) – which identifies the level of performance (as a CPI) required to keep to budget (either the original budget or the estimate at completion (EAC)).

USING THESE APPROACHES

The critics of earned value approaches identify a range of problems, including:

- Inadequate underpinning of the project management process, including a weak or non-existent WBS
- Lack of integration between the WBS, the project schedule and the budget
- Poor cost management (and recording) systems
- Lack of experience in using the formulae
- Weak project management and control

TRAFFIC LIGHT CONTROL

Traffic light control takes many forms. It is useful for those who have limited monitoring data.

In this approach, team members estimate the likelihood of meeting the planned target date, using the 'one traffic light' system, where they identify a colour associated with their view of performance. The colours signify:

- *Green* = 'on target', when project performance is on plan, and meeting stakeholder expectations.

- *Yellow* = 'not on target, but recoverable', when some problem areas are identified, but where corrective actions can address these problems.

- *Red* = 'not on target and recoverable only with difficulty', when there are major problems, and a major component is well off-target and could impact seriously on the project.

Traffic lights are a limited form of monitoring, as it is subjective and only highlights the stated views on non-achievement. There is no requirement to detail work done (or to be done) or to quantify expected delays.

A variation of this system is the 'triple constraint' traffic light system, using the core three elements of successful projects, that of budget, schedule and performance.

- *Green*= all three objectives substantially met to date
- *Yellow*= two of the three objectives substantially met to date
- *Red*= less than two objectives substantially met to date

The focus is commonly on Red lights activities, but consideration must be given to the impact of the delays in the 'yellow' on other activities, tasks and milestones.

ACTIVITY 20.7

Traffic light monitoring is an intuitively easy approach. How robust is this?

THE PROJECT SCORECARD

Project scorecards extend the traffic light approach to provide progress summaries on key performance metrics for a project. They are produced on a regular basis, for example weekly, monthly or quarterly, depending on the project. This scorecard approach complements, rather than replaces, other planning and monitoring systems.

Organisations must determine appropriate metrics to include in their project scorecards. These can take one of the two forms. The first focuses on key project management dimensions, including:

- *Cost*, e.g. between the actual spend against planned spend
- *Quality*, e.g. the percentage of work completed to standard
- *Time*, e.g. the extent to which the project is meeting the project schedule
- *Corporate factors*, e.g. the extent to which corporate goals or standards are being met

The second takes a 'balanced scorecard' approach, and assumes that assessing the following dimensions will deliver the above benefits:

- The financial perspective, e.g. EVA, ROI

- *The customer perspective*, customer satisfaction, economic value added. (Notice the difference between earned value analysis and economic value added. The commonality of the acronyms can cause confusion.)

- The training and innovation perspective, staff PM expertise, lessons learned

- *The project or other internal business perspective*, e.g. satisfaction indices, fit with corporate objectives

IICD, The International Institute for Communication and Development, a non-profit organisation, developed a 'project scorecard evaluation tool' to monitor its projects. IICD focuses on facilitating the development of poor communities in countries such as Bolivia, Jamaica, Mali and Uganda, through technology – ranging from radio and television to Internet solutions – in a range of sectors. This development approach requires a unique project scorecard, with customised measures.

Three broad headings were identified for this scorecard:

- *Content* – two elements were measured – project and owner success, and the development impact of the project
- *Money* – the project's financial contribution
- *Process* – how effective the IICD was in the project

Project and owner success and the project's financial contribution are monitored by quarterly progress reports from the local managers.

The development impact and IICD effectiveness are measured through research and discussion. Different questionnaires are targeted at different stakeholders, with a series of attitude statements and open-ended questions, including measuring the awareness of ICT possibilities, levels of empowerment, perceived income and employment benefits. Local project partners rated IICD's effectiveness on two dimensions – local ownership and IICD's project support.

Then, focus group meetings are held to identify how to refocus projects to enable projects to make more impact.

Source: IICD website, http://www.iicd.org/approach/monitoring_evaluation/methodology

This information can be presented in different ways. Some organisations produce a simple one-page sheet, which:

- Highlights key developments
- Shows the tracking of the key performance matrices
- Identifies areas that need attention (i.e. are over budget, late, possible risks on the horizon etc.)

The temporary nature of projects means that tracking and monitoring systems must be accessible, easy to use and current. As a temporary initiative, some or all aspects of the project tracking may not fit well within the existing information systems. Further, often only the larger projects have staff with responsibilities, for example information systems or finance. Therefore, the tracking data should be, wherever possible, gathered as part of the normal routine of the project.

Another general rule is that the reporting should be kept brief. Therefore, an updated report should be only a page or two for most projects.

CORRECTIVE ACTION PLANS

Project control often results in preparing corrective action plans. Some project managers feel that it is not really an issue that milestones are missed, but it *is* an issue when corrective plans are not made.

Corrective action plans (CAP) will have knock-on effect on all WBS activities and tasks that are subsequent to a particular milestone. Some activities and tasks may need more resources applied to them, for example hiring additional labour, in order to catch up on the schedule. Further, there may be cost penalties due to some contract workers not being used or having to be hired at late notice.

The corrective action plan needs to trade-off the costs against the schedule and the quality of the work. Interestingly, most managers focus on time and cost alone, and the outcome of the project then becomes the problem.

Making CAPs may seem a relatively simple process, but often this may not be the case, as there will be multiple demands for resources, and experience shows that there will be multiple delays or budgets being exceeded during a project. Organisations may set up a Corrective Action Planning Process to ensure that the problems do not escalate or cause further problems. Possible stages in this are:

- Identify, assess and agree on the problem
- Identify the causes of this problem
- Prioritise the problem within the project
- Develop a corrective action plan
- Gain approval for the CAP
- Execute the CAP
- Monitor and report on CAP
- Close the CAP process

CASE EXAMPLE

Sky announced a recall of more than 90,000 HD set-top boxes when a manufacturing assembly fault was identified in 10% of the boxes.

With the large number of boxes to be replaced, it is estimated that it will take more than three months to arrange appointments for a free replacement box to be fitted for all customers with faulty boxes. These customers will also be given a bonus free subscription period to compensate for the problems.

Sky records the box codes, so that it could identify customers who may have a faulty box.

Sky expected the total recall programme to cost 'seven figures'. It is negotiating with Pace, the supplier for the boxes, over who will bear the costs.

Sources: Daily Mail (2009) "Sky to replace 90,000 HD boxes after manufacturing fault is discovered", 17 February, http://www.daily-mail.co.uk/news/article-1147042/Sky-replace-90-000-HD-boxes-manufacturing-fault-discovered.html

Anon (2009), "Pace hit by Sky box glitch", Investor's Chronicle, 17 February, 2009 http://www.investorschronicle.co.uk/Companies/ByEvent/Risk/Inbrief/article/20090217/639b525a-fcf0-11dd-ac57-00144f2af8e8/Pace-hit-by-Sky-box-glitch.jsp

ACTIVITY 20.8

Refer to the Sky recall case study.

1. Identify how the progress of this recall project can be monitored?
2. How could the traffic light system be used to control progress?
3. What outcomes could trigger a change to their existing plan?
4. What corrective actions could be required?

SUMMARY

The focus of monitoring and control is not to cast blame, but to check on whether the project is still on target. If it is not, then the project manager can then try to get the project back on track.

Successful project monitoring requires a good data collection approach and communication of the results to all parties. The basic findings can be analysed if they are key performance indicators or merely because exception reporting highlights problems.

Control is when the project progress against the project plan is checked and corrective action can be taken if required. This will span across the topics that form the project plan. A range of tools can assist in this process.

Senior Examiner's Comments – Section Four

This section of the syllabus realises the dynamic evolution of the marketing function and the practical fact that organisational management and planning are presenting common denominators. Marketing projects and project management principles are inextricably linked, and a paradigm exists. Content and knowledge will be drawn from all Level 4 units, but ultimately themes and perspectives from the other three units at Level 6 will be investigated and applied.

Students should examine core project management techniques and identify the interface with the principles of marketing management. The appreciation and understanding of this relationship will allow the integration of dual concepts in a practical scenario. For marketing project plan, read marketing plan. There is little difference in format and structure, only nature and scope. It is fully expected that students arrive at this unit in no doubt as to, and fully competent in, the necessary frameworks of the marketing planning process. This is a fundamental imperative and anything less would not permit any candidate to undertake this unit, let alone be successful in it. These frameworks will be adapted to fit any given organisational context or brief.

This section in turn becomes the marketing project plan and is built from the study and application of the content from the previous three sections.

Candidates will therefore be expected to integrate not only their knowledge from the other units and previous study but also a coherent application of the concepts and frameworks specifically introduced here.

Having arrived at a justified position for the project, the student will now formulate the initiation, the progression, the measurement and the completion of a contextualised marketing project.

The core content of this section is clearly defined and should be used as a template for what becomes the project document. What will emerge is a cumulative and summative understanding and practical application of a concept for managing marketing projects.

There is nothing here that is trying to be overcomplicated for overcomplication's sake. The syllabus is clearly defined and indicative content outlined.

The examining team will expect nothing less than the consequential and structured approaches referred to by Element 4.3 of the syllabus document.

This element of the assessment carries the most individual weight in relation to the marking criteria, representing up to a quarter of the total mark. This task will always form a part of the candidate's brief, and the full remit within a project plan should always be used. The examiners will be expecting an all-inclusive presentation of the situational context, formalised and quantified objectives, operational delivery and implementation programmes, dedicated timescales, investment/income budgets and monitoring, evaluation and measurement mechanics. Anything less is unlikely to be accepted.

- A core understanding of and an ability to apply traditional project management techniques in any given context are imperative here.

Bibliography for Section 4

Baker, B. (2008) Filling the gaps. *PM Network*, 22(6), 26–27.

Brown, C.J. (2000) The dimensions of a project management supporting organisational culture. Paper presented to the World Project Management Week Conference, Queensland, Australia.

Burke, R. (2003) *Project Management: Planning and Control*. John Wiley & Sons, Chichester.

Cooper, M.J., Gwin, C.F. and Wakefield, K.L. (2008) Cross-functional interface and disruption in CRM projects: Is marketing from Venus and information systems from Mars? *Journal of Business Research*, 61(4), 292–299.

Dean, B.V. (1968) *Evaluating, Selecting, and Controlling R&D Projects*, AMA Research Study 89. American Management Association, Inc.

Hickens, M. (2008) Day late and a dollar Shai. *eWeek*, 25(14), 9–10.

Kapur, and Gopal, K. (2004) Intelligent disobedience. *Computerworld*, 38(35), pp. 38–38

Kezsbom, D.S. (2001) People issues. *AACE International Transactions*, 1–2.

Maylor, H. (2005) *Project Management*. John Wiley & Sons, Harlow.

Meredith, J.R. and Mantell, S.J. (2000) *Project Management: A Managerial Approach*. John Wiley & Sons, New York.

Meredith, J.R. and Mantell, S.J. (2003) *Project Management: A Managerial Approach*. John Wiley & Sons, New York.

Obeng, E. (1994) *All Change! The Project Leader's Secret Handbook Englewood Cliffs*. Prentice Hall, New Jersey.

Project Management Institute Standards Committee (PMI) (1996) *A Guide to the Project Management Body of Knowledge*. Project Management Institute, Upper Darby, Pennsylvania.

PMI (2004) *A Guide to the Project Management Body of Knowledge (PMBOK® Guide)*, 3rd edition. Project Management Institute.

Rad, P.F. and Levin, G. (2008) What Is Project Portfolio Management. *AACE International Transactions*, 1–4.

Saunders, J., Wong, V., Stagg, C. and Fontan, M.M.S. (2005) How screening criteria change during brand development. *Journal of Product and Brand Management*, 14(4), 239–249.

Standish Group (1994) The CHAOS Report, The Standish Group International, Inc.

Standish Group (2004) The CHAOS Report, The Standish Group International, Inc.

Wheatley, M. (2005) The road to results, *PM Network*, 19(9), 36–43.

WEB SOURCE

Anon (2009) http://www.btt-research.com

EXTENDING KNOWLEDGE

Books

Gray, C.F. and Larson, E.W. (2008) *Project Management: The Managerial Process*, 4th edition. McGraw-Hill, London.

Feedback Section

INTRODUCTION

This section contains brief outlines that should help guide your answers for the many activities throughout this book. Although the significant majority has been included, some have been deliberately left out to encourage you to enter into a dialogue with your tutor.

Remember that they are only guidelines and would need to be expanded upon in formal assessment work.

ACTIVITY 13.1

Each World Cup is a separate event, as a different football association in a different country and with different participants hosts it. There are differences in the host countries, the venues and the teams and matches, from competition to competition. However, MasterCard's experience in sponsoring football events can help in understanding processes, timescales and other issues, and to reduce the uncertainty. It will have experience in working with trusted suppliers.

There would be higher output uncertainty for an organisation with no previous experience of this event, but possibly one reason for the switch of sponsor was that FIFA did not believe MasterCard had met FIFA's desired outcomes from the sponsorship. Experience of sponsorship of other major sports events will help VISA, and would have been considered as part of the decision to award VISA the sponsorship contract. Some generic processes could be common between football and golf events, but each event has its unique characteristics. Often, companies seek to reduce input uncertainty by hiring specialists with proven track records.

ACTIVITY 13.2

Clearly, the answer to this question will depend on your business. However, you should be looking for examples and issues to help you with your studies.

For example:

If there is an organisation-wide approach to project management, you need to find out about this. Who is responsible for training and communications about this? Is there a circulation list for information on new initiatives? Is it for intra- or interdepartmental projects, or both? Are people running projects happy with this approach? Who monitors the use of this approach and how?

If there is no organisation-wide approach, then you need to find out whether individuals or departments have particular approaches, and what types of projects are undertaken. How is success of these projects measured? How do people learn how to manage projects? Is time allocated for project management, or is it just part of normal job responsibilities?

You do not need to have all the answers just now. But as the assessment for this topic is based on undertaking a project in your work environment, you need to have a general understanding of project management approaches in your organisation.

ACTIVITY 13.4

Again, your answers will vary depending on the projects undertaken within your organisation.

If you can find case studies of successful projects, identify what made them successful. Was the process well defined or implemented? Or was it the outcome of the project?

Equally, try to find out about unsuccessful projects. Why were they unsuccessful? Are there any lessons to be learnt here?

ACTIVITY 13.5

Once again, your answer will depend on your organisation. But, by now, you should be clear about the difference between routine activities and projects. You should be able to consider the uncertainty levels in your projects and know what forms of uncertainty exist.

Projects differ from routine work in their uniqueness and the resultant uncertainty. Managing this is a key to success.

Some of your projects may be adaptations of earlier projects. These still need project management, but there may be a fairly well-developed process, and your role may be to follow this. Large, new, complex projects may change between projects. You may be involved in managing these or contributing to them. In the latter case, you will be reporting to a project manager.

For your assessed project, look at the above criteria. You need to have a manageable project, which can be completed within the timeframe. Think carefully about what is realistic.

ACTIVITY 13.6

Some organisations do not distinguish well between these different types of projects. This can result in poor use of management and administrative time.

The Amgen case shows that often it is the smaller routine projects that are harder to deal with, if the organisation does not support these appropriately.

ACTIVITY 13.7

The Pepsi case shows a strategic project – probably one of the most substantial ones that could be undertaken.

There is one 'master' project, but in each country, brand, type of activity (e.g. merchandising, trade marketing and advertising).

These must ultimately all link together. Once the master project is agreed, then all the smaller components would automatically have priority. However, the WAY in which these are delivered in each market, for each brand, would have to be approved (i.e. have a business case for a specific subproject). Your project may be one of these smaller projects that are part of a bigger project.

ACTIVITY 14.1

Hopefully, you will not have any – or too many – of these!

Some of these will come to fruition – and some will be successful and some will not. The challenge is that these pet projects could show real insight (like Sony's Akio Morita, the Walkman) or be heading for a disaster (like the infamous Ford Edsel). Few organisations nowadays can survive the disasters.

It is probably not ideal to have one of these as your assessed project. You may not have the chance to show your knowledge to best effect, and if its sponsor leaves, your project may 'collapse'.

ACTIVITY 14.2

Hopefully, you will be able to find some evidence of evaluation of projects. Try to find out about the criteria that are used and when (e.g. is there a schedule for this evaluation – such as around the time that budgets are submitted) these are reviewed.

You may find a mix of both planned projects (which could be related to investment decisions, or promotional objectives, for example), and those that are necessitated by changing market opportunities, and those that are considered independently. The latter may need funding from some contingency fund.

You will have to justify the project that is the focus of your CIM assessment, even if there is no internal assessment process. So take time to think about this topic and apply to your project.

ACTIVITY 14.3

The repositioning project initiation stage is likely to have started before the consultants were appointed for the evaluation project. In other words, this is a part of a bigger project. It is likely that this is the first stage in the implementation of this project. The work undertaken in a project only becomes visible to people outside the organisation once the project implementation starts.

ACTIVITY 14.4

It is commonly assumed that marketing staff can become capable project managers, but that is not always the case. Some marketing managers are poor at working with others, keeping to budgets and schedules etc. Good project managers work at this. Developing project management skills can – as the IBM case shows – make a better manager, in many disciplines. You may find that additional training and/or mentoring could help you develop skills and competencies in these areas.

ACTIVITY 14.5

The project scope and objectives helps all participants stay focused on the project and its objectives. Moving beyond this increases the cost, timescales, and can impact on the performance and customer satisfaction. (The importance of these elements was identified in previous chapters.)

The deliverables (i.e. the desired outcomes or results) should also be specified. Explanation of the project outcomes helps team members have a clear understanding of what the output should be.

The project management methodologies to be used detail how the project will stay on schedule and to cost, and integrate the different project activities. They also provide guidance and progress reports for all participants.

Any constraints or limiting factors, such as time, money, people or equipment, weather conditions and cultural problems, highlight factors that set the parameters for work, and also identify issues that have to be considered in the management of the project.

Any potential risks in the project and details about how these are going to be managed and monitored help organisations determine the potential problems and losses from this project.

The overall budget for the project is clearly a critical dimension to ensure that the project does not overspend, and delivers value for money.

ACTIVITY 14.6

Clearly, Volvo team briefed the agency on the project, and worked with them to develop a more specific project scope, outcome and objectives. There would be a process of collaboration between the agency and Volvo, although usually the client company is not involved in the day-to-day aspects of campaign development.

However, the local adaptation of this campaign involves collaboration with local Volvo markets, as well as the corporate marketing teams.

Local markets would see a general overview of the campaign and the specific schedules for their markets. This enables them to see the context, but to focus on what is appropriate for their markets.

ACTIVITY 15.1

Advertising, field marketing, research agencies etc. are commonly project-oriented organisations. Review the characteristics of project-oriented organisations and compare them with the agencies you work for or with.

Traditionally managed organisations are typically less supportive of project work. Often, organisations have not changed radically, and managers are more comfortable with a traditional hierarchical form of management.

However, there is growing evidence that POO can help project success, and support projects, and that they recognise the importance of projects in the organisation's success. Failing projects (those that do not meet objectives, time or budgets) often face internal organisational support and commitment barriers.

ACTIVITY 15.2

If you are in a POO, then it is likely that you have more support for projects, and this may include your assessed project. Traditionally structured organisations often require project managers to spend more time negotiating for resources – including staff time – to be available for your project.

ACTIVITY 15.3

Often, organisations use the same approach to forming teams, and sometimes they exclude external parties. Project orientation approaches encourage the involvement of all stakeholders, which can include agencies, and strive for flexibility, which may explain why Nokia uses freelancers.

ACTIVITY 15.4

If you found it difficult to answer this, you need to start looking in the marketing trade press or financial pages of newspapers to get better awareness of good examples. Learning from best practice is critical in marketing.

Companies like Apple are often described as being innovative. Typically, these companies have a strong company culture, and often have fervour and enthusiasm for the company and its products. The company is less 'mechanistic' (highly structured) and more 'organic' (fluid, or changing).

People at all levels can feed into company decisions. Note that Apple can still have strong leadership.

A few years ago, Marks and Spencers was seen as an example of a company that was failing to evolve with the market. It was characterised by being hierarchical and led from the top. Store-based staff claimed that they were not encouraged to come up with new ideas or listened to.

The Apple culture fosters new ideas and change towards what the company stands for, and in doing so, it gets more from – and rewards – its people. Staff at M&S said that they were demotivated, and customers were disappointed.

Which of these is most like your organisation? And what are the implications of this for your assessed work?

ACTIVITY 15.5

The Project Management team is the agency account team (planning and creative people), but the management of Land Rover are the project owners. It is the agency's responsibility to ensure that the advertising meets the task within the time and budget.

This form of briefing engaged the team, helping them understand the potential of the Land Rovers and Range Rovers. By experiencing the vehicles, they were able to understand differentiation and added-value aspects of the product, and the excitement from using the vehicles. This better communicated the goals for the advertising campaign than a written brief, and motivated the team.

Kevin Eikenberry offers team-commitment-building programmes based on the CARB model:

Commitment to the team and each other
Alignment and goal agreement
Relationships among team members
Behaviours and skills needed to reach performance goals

For further information, visit http://www.kevineikenberry.com/.

ACTIVITY 15.6

A marketing or business qualification was the preferred academic background, coupled with business experience. The business experience sought encompassed a range of areas related to the role. These included having experience in leading and executing marketing projects.

ACTIVITY 15.7

Just check – have you considered these operations people as customers, and used the language they understand and examples that relate to their situation?

ACTIVITY 16.1

One of the most consistent feedback comments on CIM students' work is 'lack of focus on the set question'. This means that the students have failed to identify what is required to achieve the top marks.

A second criticism is that students have written 'an all you know answer', which means that students have seen a key topic in the question or task and then written 'all they have studied and learnt' on this topic, without consideration of its fit to the question.

The latter has two problems. First, selectivity is (either implicitly or explicitly) an assessment criterion. Lack of selectivity then loses marks.

Second, where time or word count is limited, focusing on the less relevant means that there is less on what really matters.

The same issue applies to projects. If you focus on what you already know, or what you think is interesting, you will not use time and resources well.

ACTIVITY 16.3

This feedback will address the second of these two projects. All comments here are based only on the scope statements indicated.

Activities could include:

Identifying the key marketing disciplines, such as research, segmentation, planning etc.

Defining the game approach
Developing content

Outside the scope of this could include:
Offering online tutorials
Producing textbooks

Areas that are not clear:
Is this to be a computer-based game or a board game?
Is it for the staff or managers?

ACTIVITY 16.4

There are many problems when project scope is poorly defined. These include:
Lack of focus
Lack of control over the budget
Internal politics problems
Poor outcomes
Constant changes in the project
Lack of responsibility
Late delivery
High costs

ACTIVITY 16.5

Basically, this is a rather substantial insult. It says that the company is not professional in managing its implementation, as it expands the project.

Scope creep and late delivery are usually closely linked. Interestingly, it may not be the commissioning company that will carry the financial penalties.

ACTIVITY 17.1

This is absolutely NOT the case. A longer task is a more complex task. Complexity increases the time involved. Further, this task usually has developmental or reflective issues. These require time to review.

Take this advice, and build in contingencies into your assignment project plan!

ACTIVITY 17.2 (AND 17.3)

The answer here depends on your approach. Interestingly, you may have already laid this out in the order of the contents of the section on Gantt charts and critical paths.

If you have not done this already, try it after reading the next sections, and note how the two different types of approach treat predecessor and successor tasks.

ACTIVITY 18.1

You will get some clues if you read the article. Kotler says:

This (putting the stoppers on the projects) is not the answer. It is better to keep investing, or work smarter.

This is the central issue – projects should be continued or culled on their individual merits. Therefore, the project must be considered in terms of the fit with strategy and the returns on the project. A good project will have these specified at the outset. These should be reviewed throughout the process as these may be required to defend your project in events of cutbacks.

ACTIVITY 18.2

Although the project cost appears to be facing approximately 10% increase in cost, and a critical timing delay that will adversely affect some stakeholders (the retailers and the shoppers), it is likely that the project will continue.

This demonstrates why many project budgets increase, and also why deadlines are not met – there are different stakeholder interests, which impact on the project process, but often projects continue in spite of these and cost and timing problems. This is especially common in major public sector costs, especially following considerable initial investment.

However, these factors can cause ill will after the end of the project, and therefore affect the project when it moves into the implementation stage. You will see discussion of this later in the chapter in relation to the Millennium Dome.

ACTIVITY 18.3

The project appears to have met the project deadline and budget set. It seems to be functionally achieving what it was set up to deliver. In project management terms, this met the requirements.

However, the purpose of this project was to move people away from using the call centres, and this implementation level did not happen immediately. The users found that the routing – the number of actions to get to information or to perform tasks – was slow. A further review and development was needed five months after launch. The management was unhappy, and felt that the project had failed to meet the required levels of acceptance, which in turn meant that partners could not get the promised margin increase.

Interestingly, the adoption of this was found to follow the pattern of new product diffusion. The original expectations for an early switch to the website were overstated.

ACTIVITY 18.4

The stakeholders for the Millennium Dome included the UK population, politicians, suppliers, tour operators, employees, international tourists etc. Their needs differed, but most needed the project to be completed on time and on budget. The UK people were less concerned about the project deadline as long as the subsequent operation was well managed. The Media were also important stakeholders, and should have been managed within the process.

The project management life cycle for the Millennium Dome project began with the initiation of the concept, and identification of a site, and finished when the project was complete. Practically, this was when the Dome opened on 31 December, 1999. The later project reviews finished the project management activity.

The Millennium Dome project was a success in opening on time, but a failure in that it exceeded its budgets and also lost support in key stakeholder groups, which subsequently damaged its potential to operate as a profitable venture.

ACTIVITY 19.2

GE's managers had a toolbox, or a series of processes to manage different situations. This ensured consistent management systems for controlling performance and productivity. 3M's 'sandbox' approach was somewhat more playful, aiming to nurture creativity, and showing less accountability and focus on performance than at GE. GE's business focus ensures that resources are used to best advantage. 3M's approach works fine as long as the creative environment produces successful innovations. However, while 3M had considerable innovation success for many years, it is clear that this approach may not deliver the required returns. McNerney tried to combine GE's business systems, and an environment to encourage innovation.

Introducing new tools changed the focus of 3M's innovation process. While previously this was unfocused (the analogy with a sandbox relates to the innovation process being 'fun' and about 'playing'), the GE mentality was focused on outcomes that would generate profit. This fits with managing performance, cost and delivery in their new product development processes.

However, while clearly McNerney had to take action to improve focus, it is possible that some of the 'good' aspects of 3M's process could be removed from this focus.

ACTIVITY 19.3

This is a simplified description of the methodology. However, while scope is allowed to change, it is within defined parameters. It is more focused on outputs rather than the processes to deliver outputs. It is used in fast-moving environments, where failing to change the project because of external changes (or other learning) would lead to project termination.

ACTIVITY 20.1

Often, project plans focus on the 'hard issues' rather than the 'soft issues'. So commonly, people issues are not included in the project plan. These include monitoring stakeholder attitudes, including the commitment of the project team members. Too often, the focus is on measuring what is available rather than what is important.

ACTIVITY 20.2

This depends on the nature of your project. However, you should review your original plans later in the project, and identify whether your approach was followed and how well it worked.

You should refer to your other studies on holding meetings to ensure that project meetings are handled correctly.

Common problems with reporting include data and reporting overload, which gets in the way of project progress. At the other extreme, sometimes getting the required data and information is difficult, especially if some or all data is in a central 'enterprise' system, which may have boundary or analysis constraints.

ACTIVITY 20.3

With 300 sales people to be trained and 93 who have undergone the training programme, the progress (for this 'work package') is 31% complete (93/300).

With a total budget for this work package of £60,000, the earned value (of this 'work package') is £18,600. This means that there is a variance between the budget for the work scheduled and the proportionate costs.

Variance analysis identifies costs problems. These can break down the costs further, to identify the major influences on cost variations whether the project budget is under threat. It could be that there was a cost of preparing training materials or that there were higher travelling expenses for the first people through training.

If all these are taken into account, it could be that other factors have changed and that action may need to be taken to ensure that the project is completed on time and to cost. These latter aspects show the shift from monitoring to controlling a project.

ACTIVITY 20.5

The first problem is that this has damaged the relationship between the JV partners, as Danone is the majority partner, and that they are not benefiting from these unauthorised sales.

Second, their reputation was damaged by a campaign by the owner of Wahaha in China, and Danone's sales in Asia have dropped.

The company is still in dispute in 2009. Clearly, this has cost the company dearly. The company probably spotted this problem, but rather late in the day. It should have been understood in the initial JV development project.

Danone's response to the Dickinson article is available at:

http://www.chinaeconomicreview.com/cer/2007_09/Fact_Sheet_-_the_Dispute_with_Mr_Zong_Qinghou.html

ACTIVITY 20.6

Cost Performance Index: Cost performance index (CPI) = Earned value (EV)/Actual cost (AC).

On the basis of the answer to the earlier question, this is £18,500 divided by £24,000, which is 77. This means that every pound of the budge is only generating 83 pence in earned value.

To calculate the CPI two months later, you need to first identify the EV.

As 150 of the 300 sales people have undergone training, training is 50% complete.

The EV is therefore £30,000, against the AC of £33,000.

The CPI is then £30,000/£33,000, which is 0.91.

The increase in the CPI shows that every pound spent on the project created 91 pence of value. Therefore, progress is in the right direction for this project.

ACTIVITY 20.7

This depends very much on the experience of the people involved in delivering on tasks, in understanding the work involved and in being realistic about the potential for delivering to target. The reliability of this depends on trust within the team.

ACTIVITY 20.8

1. Clearly, this will require access to the company's customer and operations records, to identify which customers are affected, whether they have been contacted, whether an appointment has been set and whether their boxes have been replaced.
2. A traffic light system could be used at each of these stages, but this would need to be based on hard data of performance against targets. It may be better to use some of the other quantitative analyses identified earlier, given the value of this activity.
3. Failing to be able to contact customers or failing to be able to schedule appointments could cause problems. Further problems with set-top boxes, or reduced labour available for replacing the boxes (for whatever reasons) could cause a change to plans.
4. There are many possible actions, which would depend on the problems facing the company. If there is no real urgency, it might be possible to go beyond the existing schedule. However, if the schedule is critical, it might be necessary to hire contract telemarketing teams to help contact customers, or have special contract teams to do changeover of the boxes. This would add to the cost.

Index